BURGER NIGHT

BUR
HIE

Deborah Kaloper

60+ RECIPES FOR DATE NIGHTS,
LAZY NIGHTS AND PARTY NIGHTS

Smith
Street
Books

INTRODUCTION

How did an unassuming beef steak from the German port of Hamburg become one of the world's favourite foods?

Today you can pick up a hamburger in the most remote corners of the globe, from street stalls in bustling hill towns, to gourmet restaurants in five-star hotels. You can feast on teriyaki burgers in Tokyo and juicy, herbed lamb burgers in Monaco, add kimchi to your patty in Korea, or smother it with 'the lot' (beetroot, pineapple and perhaps a fried egg) in Sydney. Don't eat meat? Enjoy an aloo tikki burger in Agra, or black bean slider in Berlin.

The story of the burger is one of nostalgia, accidental genius and some sizzling competition – at least 40 places in the United States claim they 'served it here first'. The original Hamburg steak was a simple patty of minced beef, served for dinner on the steamer ships bringing German immigrants from Hamburg to New York in the late 1800s. It became hugely popular onboard as a comforting reminder of home – it was well-seasoned, and sometimes came with a pile of onions.

By the middle of the twentieth century, however, that simple patty had become a culinary marvel – the very symbol of the American dream. So, how did it find itself in a toasted brioche bun, piled high with crisp iceberg lettuce and creamy slaw, sour–salty dill pickles, irresistibly gooey melted cheese and an array of addictive specially made 'special' sauces?

The lightbulb moment came at the 1904 World's Fair in St Louis, with the genius thought: 'Hey, what if we put this meat patty on bread?' Presumably so it could be eaten with one hand, while the other kept a tight grip on the newly released Harley-Davidson.

It was simple but revolutionary, turning the hamburger into a quick and easy-to-eat snack that everyone could enjoy on the go. And, at the start of the twentieth century, everyone was 'on the go' … there were a whole lot of skyscrapers to be built and Model T Ford production lines to be staffed.

Things got serious in 1921, when a shiny clean 'fast food' kitchen called White Castle opened in Wichita, Kansas, serving 'sliders'. This tiny square meat patty (yes: square!) in its tiny square bun was the burger that spawned many a fast-food empire. Indeed, in 2014 *Time* magazine named it the 'most influential burger' of all time.

White Castle expanded across the States, making burgers that were comfortingly identical every time. They were good value, fast and easy to eat while holding your soda – or steering your new production-line car. Burger cravings became a thing.

In 1934 a Kentucky restaurant melted a slice of cheese over a meat patty and the word 'cheeseburger' entered the dictionary. Around 1950, New York's swanky 21 Club put one on its menu, simultaneously shocking local patrons and inventing the 'gourmet burger'. (Today, the world's most luxurious burger is the Golden Boy. Made with wagyu beef, caviar and a gold-leaf bun, it will set you back about US$6000.)

In 1957 two big burger chains introduced their rival quarter-pounders, and in 1981 a veggie burger at an Oregon restaurant quickly became the most popular item on the menu.

The burger is now so ubiquitous it serves as an informal measure of the economy – as seen in *The Economist* magazine's Big Mac index.

While success in the fast-food world came about through the burger's reassuring nostalgic consistency, its real kitchen joy lies in its versatility. The beef patty still reigns supreme, but you can build a burger around a chicken or eggplant parma, stacked rings of crumbed calamari, a juicy portobello mushroom, or fillet of marinated crisp-skin salmon.

This is a feast that can be eaten anywhere, everywhere and any time.

Home alone? Surely the classic tuna melt – crunchy with potato chips and dill pickles – is the best late-night snack ever? No judgement. Drinks party? Hand around sliders filled with Italian meatballs or prawn cocktail. Friends round? Make yourself famous for your gochujang-glazed KFC. (Or have an Elvis night: the King couldn't go past a southern fried chicken waffle with sweet 'n' spicy hot syrup.) Dinner party? Go gourmet, with pulled duck and pickled slaw in toasted milk buns, or a New England lobster burger, with homemade herbed mayonnaise. Fancy adding crispy bacon rashers, onion rings or a fried egg? As long as you can fit it in your mouth, Elvis, the choices are all yours.

BURGER ESSENTIALS

MEAT PATTIES

Your bun might contain a veggie burger or fish fillet, but if it's holding a meat patty, there are some basic rules for success. Firstly, the patty should be slightly larger than your bun, so it doesn't disappear from view inside. Secondly, press an indent in the centre of each patty with your thumb before cooking – that way it will stay flat and not dome up.

BEEF

The aim is for a flavourful hamburger that holds together well, stays juicy and tender, and doesn't dry out as it cooks. Minced (ground) beef is the classic choice, but not all beef is created equal. You want to avoid lean cuts here – the fat is what gives the burger its juiciness. Freshly ground beef is best (ask your butcher to grind it for you, if that's available, or do it yourself at home).

The golden ratio is 80 per cent meat to 20 per cent fat, depending on how you're cooking the patty. If you're grilling, a higher fat content will keep your burgers juicy. If you're pan-frying, you can get away with using slightly leaner meat, under 20 per cent fat.

Chuck steak offers the ideal balance of meat and fat – plus it's flavourful, tender and relatively inexpensive. Some burger aficionados like to mix it with different cuts for flavour, such as brisket, short rib or sirloin. Either way, freshly ground chuck is a reliable starting point.

PORK & LAMB

Minced (ground) pork naturally has a fat content of around 17 per cent, which is perfect. Don't buy 'lean pork mince' for burgers.

Just as with beef, for the juiciest burgers use lamb with a fat content of around 20 per cent.

CHICKEN & TURKEY

You'll find most chicken burgers use a marinated piece of chicken thigh or breast, because ground chicken mince is very lean. This, of course, makes it a lighter, healthier option, but you need to take care your burger patties aren't dry. That's why juicy ingredients, such as cheese and breadcrumbs are often added to the patty mix.

Turkey has a 93 to seven per cent meat to fat ratio, so is similarly very lean.

KEY INGREDIENTS

BREAD BUNS

The patty might try to hog all the glory, but a great burger needs a good bun. Don't let your pile-it-high creation fall apart because of inferior crumbly bread – there are plenty of sturdy, great-flavoured options around. However, the classic hamburger bun – white, brown, seeded or vegan – still has its place, and this is definitely it!

Your bun should be a tiny bit smaller than the patty, so it hugs it lovingly, rather than smothering it into obscurity. And lightly toast the bun for crunch – otherwise you're just making a sandwich.

BRIOCHE BUN

Ooh la la! Originally used for desserts, French brioche dough is buttery soft, dense and slightly sweet. The combination of juicy meaty patty with subtly sweet bread has proven irresistible – the brioche bun is now a crowd favourite.

POTATO BUN

Strong and sturdy, yet airy and light, the potato bun keeps it all together to the very last bite, even when you've piled the fillings high. Potato flakes are added to the dough along with potato flour, so it's subtly sweet. There are usually good vegan and dairy-free versions available.

MILK BUN

More savoury than sweet (compared to the brioche bun), the distinctively flavoured milk bun (yes – it tastes milky!) is even softer than a potato bun, but with a crisper crust. Structurally sturdy, yet still melt-in-your-mouth, the milk bun has the magical quality of being able to absorb sauces without becoming soggy.

KAISER ROLL

Originally from Austria, but now baked across the world, this round crusty roll has a soft centre. It's smaller than other rolls, so a great choice for hand-held party burgers.

CIABATTA OR FOCACCIA ROLL

If your fully loaded burger with multiple sauces is proving too much for a more traditional bun, swap to a robust ciabatta roll. Toast before filling, so it's crunchy rather than chewy.

CHEESE ...
AMERICAN-STYLE

Iconic American-style cheese knows its place – and that's on a cheeseburger. It melts into a deliciously gooey, velvety blanket over a juicy meat patty faster than you can say 'cheddar' ... But is it really cheese? Technically, it's 'processed cheese' – made by blending cheese with a few other ingredients, such as sodium citrate. Invented by Kraft Foods in the 1910s, its superpower is perfect meltability. It's not trying to be fancy or complex: it's there for comfort and nostalgia. If you prefer something less processed, there are plenty of other options.

CHEDDAR

This hard, full-fat cow's milk cheese is one of the best and most popular alternatives to 'American-style'. It goes well with everything, has a great melty texture and a sharper flavour than American-style cheese.

MONTEREY JACK

Famous for its great melting ability, Monterey Jack is another excellent cheeseburger choice. Its relatively mild taste is great with bold flavours. 'Jack' was originally made in Monterey, California.

PEPPER JACK

Similar to Monterey Jack, but its melty gooeyness comes with a fiery kick thanks to added spicy peppers.

GRUYERE

This nutty-flavoured, sweet, hard cheese is made in Switzerland from the milk of cows grazed on Alpine pastures. Pale yellow and with small holes, it melts so well that it's traditionally used for the national dish: fondue.

GOUDA

Semi-hard and creamy in taste, with a small number of holes and a red-wax coating similar to Edam, this traditional Dutch cheese is also great for burgers. Bold, smoky gouda holds its own with barbecue sauce.

HAVARTI

With its creamy, buttery flavour, this semi-hard Danish cow's cheese is easily sliced and has excellent meltability.

MOZZARELLA

Fresh, semi-soft Italian cheese made from cow's milk with a sweet, mild, milky flavour, mozzarella is great for melting – which is why it's used on pizzas and pastas as well as for cheeseburgers. Scamorza (smoked mozzarella) has a stronger flavour.

PROVOLONE

Springy, sliceable, semi-firm provolone is traditional with Italian flavours. It's great for a mild and melty cheese layer on Italian meatball sliders.

GOAT'S CHEESE

Also sold as chèvre, goat's cheese is extremely soft and spreadable. It adds a creamy, luxurious tang to a cheeseburger, and works well with caramelised onions or chutney.

TOPPINGS

Burger purists aim for contrasting layers of both flavour and texture – maybe something creamy, something tart and something crunchy, or perhaps a sweeter sauce to offset the umami burger. So, how to load it? Slather the base with sauce, top with crunchy salad and maybe a creamy slaw, add your patty or protein, and some tangy–sour pickles. Perhaps just one more dollop of sauce before you pop the bun top on?

SALAD

Crispy iceberg lettuce, juicy tomato, crunchy cucumber and, if you're in Australia, sweet yet tangy beetroot. It's not rocket science; it's burger science. You're adding texture, freshness and contrast to that juicy umami burger, glossy gooey cheese and comforting bread bun.

SAUCES

Think the basics: great mustard (American, hot English, dijon), ketchup, barbecue or chilli sauce … And then think gourmet and make your own. If burger night is how you're going to feed your friends, then nail that creamy mayo, salsa verde, blue cheese dressing, aioli or 'special sauce' and watch your burgers hit iconic status.

SLAW

Crunchy with cabbage, yet soothingly creamy with mayonnaise in the same bite, slaw is utterly perfect to be spooned over a savoury burger patty. Rainbow slaw is the colourful version. Or you might go for a spicy slaw or chopped kimchi.

PICKLES

Dill pickles are sweet yet vinegar–tart, salty but sour, soft yet kind of crunchy, and an addictive match for a juicy burger, melted cheese and soft bun. Make your own. They're incredibly easy. Make them your 'thing'.

SPECIAL SAUCE

CONDIMENTS

125 g (½ cup) Mayonnaise (see below)
or vegan mayonnaise

2 tablespoons ketchup

2 tablespoons sweet pickle relish,
or to taste

1 tablespoon American mustard

½ teaspoon white vinegar

½ teaspoon smoked paprika

¼ teaspoon garlic powder

¼ teaspoon onion powder

pinch of cayenne pepper (optional)

Pop all the ingredients into a bowl and whisk to combine. The sauce will keep in a sealed glass jar in the fridge for 7–10 days.

MAYONNAISE

CONDIMENTS

2 eggs

1 egg yolk

2 teaspoons dijon mustard

2 teaspoons white wine vinegar

¼ teaspoon sea salt

225 ml (7½ fl oz) neutral-tasting
vegetable oil

In the jug of a stick blender, blitz together the eggs, egg yolk, mustard, vinegar and salt. Slowly add the oil while blitzing, until fully emulsified. Taste, then season as desired. The mayo will keep in a sealed glass jar in the fridge for up to 10 days.

TARTAR SAUCE

▚▚▚▚▚▚▚▚▚▚▚▚▚▚▚ **CONDIMENTS** ▚▚▚▚▚▚▚▚▚▚▚▚▚▚▚

250 g (1 cup) Mayonnaise
(see opposite)

3 tablespoons finely chopped
cornichons

2–3 tablespoons finely chopped
French shallot

1 tablespoon lemon juice

1 tablespoon finely chopped parsley

1 tablespoon finely chopped dill

2 teaspoons baby capers, rinsed

1 teaspoon lemon zest

sea salt and cracked black pepper,
to taste

Place all the ingredients in a bowl and mix to combine. The sauce will keep in a sealed glass jar in the fridge for up to 1 week.

TAHINI GARLIC YOGHURT SAUCE

▚▚▚▚▚▚▚▚▚▚▚▚▚▚▚ **CONDIMENTS** ▚▚▚▚▚▚▚▚▚▚▚▚▚▚▚

125 g (½ cup) Greek-style yoghurt

65 g (¼ cup) tahini

2 tablespoons lemon juice

2–3 garlic cloves, to taste, minced

1 tablespoon finely chopped mint
leaves

sea salt and cracked black pepper,
to taste

pinch of Aleppo pepper (see Note)

Place all the ingredients in a bowl and whisk to combine. The sauce will keep in a sealed glass jar in the fridge for 5–7 days.

NOTE

Aleppo pepper is a moderately spicy chilli pepper with a complex fruity, tangy flavour that is popular in Middle Eastern cuisine.

TARTAR SAUCE

TAHINI GARLIC
YOGHURT SAUCE

TARTAR
SAUCE

SPECIAL SAUCE

MAYONNAISE

MAYO

GREEN GODDESS DRESSING

CONDIMENTS

125 g (½ cup) Greek-style yoghurt

60 g (¼ cup) Mayonnaise (page 16)

½ ripe avocado

¼ cup coriander (cilantro) leaves

1 small garlic clove, minced

2 tablespoons chopped mint leaves

2 tablespoons chopped pickled jalapeno chillies

1 tablespoon lemon juice or lime juice

sea salt and cracked black pepper

Pop all the ingredients into a blender and blitz until smooth. Taste and season with salt and pepper as desired. The dressing will keep in a sealed glass jar in the fridge for up to 5 days.

GARLIC BUTTER

CONDIMENTS

60 g (2 oz) salted butter, softened

1–2 garlic cloves, or to taste, minced

1½ teaspoons finely chopped parsley leaves

Mix all the ingredients together in a small bowl until well combined, then place in an airtight container. The butter will keep in the fridge for up to 1 week.

GRILLED ONION

CONDIMENTS

30 g (1 oz) butter
1 tablespoon olive oil
1 large onion, sliced
2 thyme sprigs
2 tablespoons Spanish sherry vinegar
1–2 teaspoons brown sugar, or to taste
good pinch of sea salt

Place a cast-iron or heavy-based frying pan over medium heat. Add the butter, olive oil, onion slices and thyme sprigs. Saute for 12–15 minutes, until the onion begins to cook down and soften. Stir in the vinegar and sugar and cook for another 5 minutes or so, until the onion starts to brown and caramelise, or is done to your liking. Stir through a good pinch of salt to finish.

The grilled onion will keep in an airtight container in the fridge for 4–5 days.

MAKES ABOUT 600 G (1 LB 5 OZ)

PICKLED RED ONION

CONDIMENTS

2 red onions, finely sliced
2 garlic cloves, finely sliced
2 red bird's eye chillies, split
2 allspice berries
1 bay leaf
¼ teaspoon black peppercorns
2 teaspoons sea salt
3 tablespoons white granulated sugar
250 ml (1 cup) apple cider vinegar
125 ml (½ cup) lime juice

Place the onion in a heatproof bowl and cover with boiling water. Let the onion sit for 20–30 seconds, then drain and refresh under cold water.

Place the onion in a large clean glass jar with the remaining ingredients, then seal and refrigerate for at least 2 hours before using.

The pickled onion will keep in the fridge for up to 2 weeks.

GRILLED ONION

GREEN GODDESS DRESSING

PICKLED RED ONION

GARLIC BUTTER

CUCUMBER RAITA

CONDIMENTS

160 g (⅔ cup) Greek-style yoghurt or coconut yoghurt

½ short cucumber, seeds removed, finely diced

1 red Asian shallot, finely diced

2 tablespoons chopped mint leaves

2 tablespoons chopped coriander (cilantro) leaves

2–3 teaspoons lime juice

1 small green chilli, finely diced

½ teaspoon ground cumin

½ teaspoon ground coriander

½ teaspoon nigella seeds

sea salt and cracked black pepper, to taste

Place all the ingredients in a bowl and mix to combine. Refrigerate in an airtight container for 4–5 days.

TZATZIKI

CONDIMENTS

2 short cucumbers, grated

1 small garlic clove, grated

½ teaspoon sea salt flakes, or to taste

2 tablespoons extra virgin olive oil

500 g (2 cups) Greek-style yoghurt

cracked black pepper, to taste

Place the grated cucumber in a clean tea towel and wrap it up tightly. Over the kitchen sink, squeeze the cucumber bundle to remove as much liquid as possible.

Transfer the cucumber to a bowl and stir through the garlic and salt. Drizzle with the olive oil, add the yoghurt and season with black pepper, then stir to combine. Use immediately or refrigerate until required.

The tzatziki will keep in an airtight container in the fridge for up to 5 days.

NAPOLI SAUCE

CONDIMENTS

2 tablespoons olive oil

1 small onion, finely diced

2 garlic cloves, minced

2 × 400 g (14 oz) tins tomatoes, crushed

1 bay leaf

2 basil sprigs

sea salt and cracked black pepper

Heat the olive oil in a large saucepan over medium heat. Add the onion and saute for 6–7 minutes, until lightly golden. Add the garlic and saute for another minute, then add the tomatoes, bay leaf and basil sprigs. Give it a good stir, then reduce the heat slightly and simmer for 20–25 minutes. Remove the bay leaf and basil sprigs, then season to taste with salt and pepper.

The napoli sauce will keep in an airtight container in the fridge for up to 5 days.

TZATZIKI

CUCUMBER RAITA

NAPOLI SAUCE

CREAMY COLESLAW

CONDIMENTS

125 g (½ cup) Mayonnaise (page 16), or more if you'd like a creamier slaw

2 tablespoons buttermilk

1 tablespoon dijon mustard

4 teaspoons apple cider vinegar

1 teaspoon honey

½ teaspoon celery seeds

225 g (3 cups) finely shredded cabbage (white or red, or a mix)

155 g (1 cup) shredded carrot

¼ red onion, finely sliced

sea salt and cracked black pepper, to taste

Place the mayonnaise, buttermilk, mustard, vinegar, honey and celery seeds in a large salad bowl and whisk to combine.

Add the cabbage, carrot and onion and toss to coat thoroughly in the dressing.

Taste and season with salt and pepper as desired. Cover and keep in the fridge; the slaw is best enjoyed the same day.

RAINBOW SLAW

CONDIMENTS

60 g (¼ cup) Mayonnaise (page 16)

1 tablespoon apple cider vinegar

2 teaspoons hot spiced honey

75 g (1 cup) shredded white cabbage

75 g (1 cup) shredded red cabbage

1 small carrot, shredded

1 spring onion (scallion), finely sliced

½ red bell pepper (capsicum), julienned

2 radishes, finely julienned

1 small jalapeno chilli, finely sliced

sea salt and cracked black pepper

Place the mayonnaise, vinegar and honey in a large bowl and whisk to combine. Add the remaining ingredients and toss to coat in the dressing.

Taste and season with salt and pepper to your liking. The slaw is best enjoyed the day it is made.

LIME PAPRIKA CREMA

▀▀▀▀▀▀▀▀▀▀▀ CONDIMENTS ▀▀▀▀▀▀▀▀▀▀▀

60 g (¼ cup) Mexican crema or
sour cream

1 tablespoon Mayonnaise (page 16)

1 small garlic clove, minced

zest of 1 lime

juice of 2–3 limes (depending on
how tangy you like it)

½ teaspoon smoked paprika

½ teaspoons chilli powder

¼ teaspoon ground cumin

Mix the ingredients in a bowl, then season to taste with salt and pepper.
Refrigerate until required.

The lime paprika crema will keep in a clean airtight container in the
fridge for 4–5 days.

MAKES ABOUT 250 G (1 CUP)

CHIPOTLE CREMA

▀▀▀▀▀▀▀▀▀▀▀ CONDIMENTS ▀▀▀▀▀▀▀▀▀▀▀

250 g (1 cup) Mexican crema, sour
cream or creme fraiche

2 chipotle chillies in adobo sauce, plus
2 teaspoons of the adobo sauce

1 tablespoon lime juice

Blitz the ingredients together in a blender and refrigerate until required.

The chipotle crema will keep in an airtight container in the fridge
for 4–5 days.

TOMATILLO SALSA VERDE

CONDIMENTS

500 g (1 lb 2 oz) tomatillos, husks removed, rinsed

½ onion

3 fresh jalapeno chillies, deseeded

3 garlic cloves

1 teaspoon sea salt

1 cup roughly chopped coriander (cilantro) leaves and stems

For a fresh salsa verde, roughly chop the tomatillos, onion and jalapenos and place in a food processor. Peel the garlic and add to the processor, along with the salt and coriander, and blend until well pureed.

For a roasted salsa verde, place the tomatillos, unpeeled onion, jalapenos and unpeeled garlic cloves on a baking tray. Place the tray under an oven grill (broiler) on high heat. Grill for 9–10 minutes, until the ingredients are slightly charred and beginning to blacken in spots, then turn them over and cook for a further 6–7 minutes, until charred. Remove from the heat and leave to cool slightly. Peel the onion and garlic, then place in a food processor with the chillies. Add the remaining ingredients and blend until pureed. Use straight away, or cool before refrigerating.

The salsa verde will keep in a glass jar in the fridge for 5–7 days.

MAKES ABOUT 625 G (2½ CUPS)

PICO DE GALLO

CONDIMENTS

3 large ripe juicy tomatoes, diced

½ white onion, diced

1 fresh jalapeno chilli, finely diced

1 small garlic clove, crushed

½ cup chopped coriander (cilantro) leaves

60 ml (¼ cup) lime juice

sea salt and cracked black pepper

Add the ingredients to a bowl and mix until well combined. Season with sea salt and black pepper to taste.

The pico de gallo is best made just before serving, but will keep in an airtight container in the fridge for 1 day.

PICO DE GALLO

CHIPOTLE CREMA

TOMATILLO SALSA VERDE

LIME PAPRIKA CREMA

QUICK-PICKLED CUCUMBER RIBBONS

CONDIMENTS

1 long cucumber, about 300 g (10½ oz), sliced into thin ribbons using a vegetable peeler or mandoline

125 ml (½ cup) white vinegar

2 tablespoons white sugar

1½ teaspoons fine sea salt

6 peppercorns

2 whole allspice berries

½ teaspoon yellow mustard seeds

Place the cucumber ribbons in a 500 ml (17 fl oz) sterilised glass jar.

In a small saucepan, warm the vinegar, 60 ml (¼ cup) of water, the sugar and salt over medium heat and stir just until the sugar dissolves. Remove from the heat and allow to cool.

Pour the cooled liquid over the cucumbers, add the spices and seal. Give the jar a little shake to distribute the spices.

Pop into the refrigerator for about 4 hours, and your pickles are ready to eat. They will keep, refrigerated, for 5–7 days.

CRISPY FRIED ONION RINGS

CONDIMENTS

1 large white onion, sliced into 1 cm (½ in) rounds, separated into rings

170 ml (⅔ cup) buttermilk

120 g (4½ oz) plain (all-purpose) flour

30 g (¼ cup) cornflour (corn starch)

1 teaspoon smoked paprika

1 teaspoon fine sea salt

½ teaspoon cracked black pepper

¼–½ teaspoon cayenne pepper, to taste

peanut oil, for deep-frying

flaked sea salt, to season

Place the onion rings and buttermilk in a bowl and toss to combine. Leave to soak for 15 minutes.

In a separate bowl, combine the flour, cornflour, paprika, salt, pepper and cayenne pepper.

Pour about 7.5 cm (3 in) of peanut oil into a large deep frying pan or saucepan and heat to 180ºC (350ºF).

Working in batches, remove a few onion rings from the buttermilk and dredge them through the spiced flour mixture, coating well. Carefully place the onion rings into the hot oil, taking care not to overcrowd the pan. Fry for about 2 minutes, until golden, crispy and cooked through, turning halfway through cooking.

Remove with a slotted spoon, drain on paper towel and sprinkle with flaked sea salt. Enjoy straight away.

CLASSIC CHEESE

BEEF

400 g (14 oz) minced (ground) beef chuck (20% fat)

400 g (14 oz) minced (ground) beef sirloin (20% fat)

1 tablespoon worcestershire sauce (optional)

1 tablespoon olive oil

sea salt and cracked black pepper

8 slices American-style cheese (see Note)

TO SERVE

4 sesame seed brioche buns, lightly toasted and buttered

Mayonnaise (page 16)

2 handfuls of shredded iceberg lettuce

sliced pickles

Special sauce (page 16)

4 red onion slices, about 5 mm (¼ in) thick

8 tomato slices

ketchup (optional)

American mustard

Place all the beef in a large bowl with the worcestershire sauce, if using. Mix to combine, then divide the meat into four equal portions and shape into patties just slightly larger than your buns. Use your thumb to make a small indentation in the centre of each patty, to help them retain their shape during cooking and prevent doming.

Heat a cast-iron frying pan or grill plate over medium–high heat and drizzle with the olive oil. Season both sides of the patties well with salt and pepper and cook for 3–4 minutes on each side, until well seared with a good caramelised crust, or until done to your liking. For the last minute of cooking, place two slices of cheese on each patty and cover with a lid to melt the cheese.

To build your burgers, slather the base buns with mayonnaise. Add the lettuce, a cheesy patty, some pickles, special sauce, a slice of onion and two slices of tomato. Drizzle with ketchup, if desired. Smear some mustard on the inside of the bun tops, place them on the burgers and enjoy.

NOTE

You can use any kind of cheese here, so pick your favourite – cheddar, Swiss, gouda, goat's cheese …

THE DOUBLE COWBOY

BEEF

1 kg (2 lb 3 oz) minced (ground) beef – equal parts chuck, boneless short rib and brisket, with 20% fat (see Note)

1 tablespoon olive oil

sea salt and cracked black pepper

8 slices monterey jack cheese, cheddar or smoky gouda (or a mix)

TO SERVE

4 hamburger buns, lightly toasted and buttered

Mayonnaise (page 16)

8 tomato slices

sliced pickled jalapeno chillies

8 slices crispy hickory-smoked bacon

Crispy fried onion rings (page 37)

smoky barbecue sauce

Divide the beef into eight equal portions and shape into patties just slightly larger than your buns. Use your thumb to make a small indentation in the centre of each patty, to help them retain their shape during cooking and prevent doming.

Heat a cast-iron frying pan or grill pan over medium heat and drizzle with the olive oil. Season the patties well with salt and pepper. Fry for 3–4 minutes on each side, until they are nicely browned and a good crust has formed, or until they are cooked to your liking. For the final minute of cooking, place a slice of cheese on each patty and cover with a lid to melt the cheese.

To build your burgers, slather the base buns with mayonnaise. Add the tomato slices and two cheesy patties to each. Top with sliced pickled jalapeno chillies, two crispy bacon slices and some fried onion rings. Drizzle on plenty of smoky barbecue sauce and finish with the bun tops.

NOTE

Ask your butcher to grind all the beef cuts for you.

THE ALL AMERICAN

BEEF

800 g (1 lb 12 oz) minced (ground) beef chuck (20% fat)

4 × 100% beef hot dogs

1 tablespoon olive oil

sea salt and cracked black pepper

8 slices American-style cheese

TO SERVE

4 sesame seed hamburger buns, split

60 g (2 oz) softened butter

Mayonnaise (page 16)

8 tomato slices

2 large handfuls of shredded iceberg lettuce

American mustard

diced white onion

sweet pickle relish

Divide the beef into four equal portions and shape into patties just slightly larger than your buns. Use your thumb to make a small indentation in the centre of each patty, to help them retain their shape during cooking and prevent doming.

Slice the hot dogs lengthways to open them out flat, but don't cut them all the way through.

Heat a large cast-iron frying pan or flat grill plate to high and drizzle with the olive oil. Season the patties well with salt and pepper, place them in the pan and cook for 3–4 minutes, until caramelised underneath with a well-browned crust. Flip them over and cook the other side for a further 2–3 minutes. For the final minute of cooking, place the cheese slices on each burger and cover with a lid to melt the cheese. Remove the burgers to a plate and keep warm.

Now cook the hot dogs for about 3 minutes, until heated through, flipping them in the pan occasionally.

To build your burgers, spread the butter over the inside of the buns, place in the hot pan and toast for 1–2 minutes, until golden brown.

Slather the base buns with mayonnaise, then top with the tomato, lettuce, a burger, a hot dog and a drizzle of mustard. Add a sprinkling of diced onion and some sweet pickle relish. Finish with the bun tops and enjoy.

DOUBLE JUICY LUCY

BEEF

800 g (1 lb 12 oz) minced (ground) beef chuck (20% fat)

1 tablespoon worcestershire sauce

10 slices American-style cheese

1 tablespoon olive oil

sea salt and cracked black pepper

TO SERVE

4 seeded hamburger buns or potato buns, lightly toasted and buttered

mustard (optional)

ketchup (optional)

4 red onion slices, about 5 mm (¼ in) thick

Mayonnaise (page 16)

Special sauce (page 16)

Place the beef in a large bowl with the worcestershire sauce. Mix to combine, then divide the meat into eight equal portions and shape into patties just slightly larger than your buns. Use your thumb to make a small indentation in the centre of each patty, to help them retain their shape during cooking and prevent doming.

Take four patties and place 1½ slices of cheese on top of each, making sure the cheese doesn't hang over the patty; if it does, simply fold the edges of the cheese slices inwards. Now add another patty on top and pinch the edges together to seal in the cheese. You now have four double 'juicy lucy' burger patties.

Heat a large cast-iron frying pan over medium–high heat and add the olive oil. Season both sides of the patties well with salt and pepper, then place into the hot pan.

Cook the patties for about 3 minutes on each side, until seared with a well-caramelised crust. For the final minute of cooking, place the remaining cheese slices on each burger and cover with a lid to melt the cheese.

To build your burgers, slather the base buns with mustard and ketchup (if using). Add the cheesy patties and red onion. Smear some mayonnaise and special sauce on the inside of the bun tops, place them on the burgers and enjoy.

CHILLI CHEESE

700 g (1 lb 9 oz) minced (ground) beef chuck (20% fat)

1 tablespoon olive oil

sea salt and cracked black pepper

CHILLI CON CARNE

1 tablespoon olive oil

1 onion, finely diced

2 garlic cloves, minced

500 g (1 lb 2 oz) minced (ground) beef (20% fat)

2½ teaspoons ground cumin

1–2 teaspoons cayenne pepper, to taste

2 teaspoons chilli powder

2 teaspoons smoked paprika

1½ teaspoons ground coriander

500 ml (2 cups) beef stock

400 g (14 oz) tin tomatoes, pureed

2 tablespoons barbecue sauce

2 chipotle chillies in adobo sauce, diced, plus 3 tablespoons of the adobo sauce

2 teaspoons worcestershire sauce

2 teaspoons sea salt

1 teaspoon cracked black pepper

TO SERVE

4 hamburger buns, lightly toasted

softened butter, for spreading

Mayonnaise (page 16)

375 g (3 cups) grated American-style cheese or cheddar

diced white onion

sliced pickled jalapeno chillies (optional)

American mustard

French fries

To make the chilli con carne, warm the olive oil in a large saucepan over medium heat and saute the onion and garlic for 5–6 minutes, until softened. Add the beef and spices, stirring and cooking until the meat has browned. Stir in the stock, tomatoes, barbecue sauce, chipotle chillies, adobo sauce and worcestershire sauce, mixing well. Bring to a rapid simmer, then reduce the heat slightly. Season with the salt and pepper and cook, stirring often, for about 2 hours, until the liquid has reduced. Taste and adjust the seasoning as desired. The sauce will keep in an airtight container in the fridge for about 5 days; gently reheat before serving.

Divide the beef into four equal portions and shape into patties just slightly larger than your buns. Use your thumb to make a small indentation in the centre of each patty, to help them retain their shape during cooking and prevent doming.

Heat a large cast-iron frying pan or flat grill to high and drizzle with the olive oil. Season the patties well with salt and pepper and cook for 3–4 minutes, until caramelised with a well-browned crust, then flip and cook the other side for a further 2–3 minutes, until done to your liking. Remove to a plate and keep warm.

To build your burgers, spread the base buns with butter, slather with mayonnaise and top with a juicy patty. Add a good amount of the chilli con carne, a handful of shredded cheese and some onion and jalapeno chilli, if using. Drizzle some mustard on the inside of the bun tops and place them on the burgers. Serve with a side of fries, topped with more chilli con carne, shredded cheese and diced onion.

DOUBLE SMASHED AVO-POBLANO CHILLI CHEESE

BEEF

520 g (1 lb 2 oz) minced (ground) sirloin beef (20% fat)

1½ teaspoons worcestershire sauce

1½ teaspoons finely chopped pickled jalapeno chillies

40 g (1½ oz) frozen salted butter, finely grated

sea salt and cracked black pepper

8 slices pepper jack or monterey jack cheese

SMASHED AVO ROASTED POBLANO CHILLI SALSA

1 large poblano chilli, about 130–150 g (4½–5½ oz)

1–2 large fresh jalapeno chillies

¼ white onion

1–2 garlic cloves, peeled

1 tablespoon extra virgin olive oil

½ ripe avocado, chopped

2 tablespoons lime juice

¼ cup coriander (cilantro) leaves

good splash of green Tabasco sauce

sea salt and cracked black pepper

TO SERVE

4 sesame seed hamburger buns, lightly toasted and buttered

Mayonnaise (page 16)

Pickled red onion (page 21)

To make the smashed avo roasted poblano chilli salsa, roast the chillies, onion and garlic under a hot grill (broiler) for 8–10 minutes in total, until charred and soft, turning halfway through. Allow to cool slightly, then peel the blistered skins from the chillies and discard. Pop the chillies, onion and garlic into a blender and give them a blitz. Add the remaining salsa ingredients and blitz again until you reach your desired salsa texture. Season to taste with salt and pepper and set aside. The sauce will keep in a sealed glass jar in the fridge for 5–7 days.

Place the beef in a large bowl with the worcestershire sauce, jalapeno chilli and butter. Mix together, then divide into eight equal portions and shape into balls. Cover and refrigerate until ready to cook; the meatballs can be shaped several hours ahead if needed.

Heat a cast-iron frying pan over high heat until very hot. Working in batches, place the balls in the pan and smash them as flat as possible, using a heavy burger press or stainless steel spatula.

Season the patties well with salt and pepper. Cook for 1–1½ minutes, until they have a good sear underneath and a well-browned crust. Flip the patties and smash down again for about 10 seconds. Season with salt and pepper, add a slice of cheese to each patty and remove when a well-caramelised crust has developed on the underside.

To build your burgers, slather the base buns with mayonnaise and add two smashed cheese patties to each. Top with the smashed avo roasted poblano chilli salsa and pickled onion. Finish with the bun tops and enjoy.

THE ITALIAN

BEEF

20 g (¼ cup) fresh soft white breadcrumbs

45 ml (1½ fl oz) milk

300 g (10½ oz) minced (ground) beef chuck (20% fat)

300 g (10½ oz) Italian fennel and chilli pork sausages, casings removed

25 g (¼ cup) finely grated parmesan

1 egg, beaten

2 garlic cloves, minced

3 tablespoons chopped basil leaves

120 g (4½ oz) mozzarella, sliced into 4 even portions

1 tablespoon olive oil

sea salt and cracked black pepper

TO SERVE

8 slices rosemary focaccia, cut slightly larger than your patties, lightly toasted

Garlic butter (page 20)

375 g (1½ cups) Napoli sauce (page 25) or store-bought napoletana pasta sauce

4 slices provolone cheese

16–20 thin pepperoni slices

finely grated parmesan

Combine the breadcrumbs and milk in a small bowl and leave to soak for about 5 minutes. Lightly squeeze out the excess milk from the breadcrumbs and discard the milk. Place the soaked bread in a large bowl with the beef, crumble in the sausage meat, then add the parmesan, egg, garlic and basil. Gently mix to combine, then divide into four equal portions and shape into balls.

Take a piece of mozzarella and stuff it into the centre of each ball, making sure it is fully encased. Shape the balls into thick patties.

Heat a cast-iron frying pan over medium–high heat. When hot, add the olive oil. Season both sides of the patties well with salt and pepper and cook for 3–4 minutes on each side, until cooked to your liking.

Meanwhile, heat the grill (broiler) to medium–high.

To build your burgers, place four toasted focaccia bread slices on a baking tray and spread with garlic butter and some of the napoli sauce. Place a patty on top with a little more napoli sauce, then a slice of provolone and the pepperoni. Pop under the grill for a few minutes, until the cheese has melted and the pepperoni is warmed and starting to crisp.

Top the burgers with a little grated parmesan, then place the other focaccia slices on top and enjoy.

THE REUBEN

600 g (1 lb 5 oz) minced (ground) beef chuck (20% fat)

40 g (¼ cup) grated onion

½ teaspoon minced garlic

1 egg, beaten

1 tablespoon olive oil

sea salt and cracked black pepper

8 slices Swiss cheese or Gruyère

10 g (⅓ oz) butter

320 g (11½ oz) shaved pastrami

TO SERVE

4 rye hamburger buns or pretzel hamburger buns

60 g (2 oz) softened butter

Russian Dressing or Thousand Island Dressing

175 g (1¼ cups) sauerkraut

dill pickles

Place the beef, onion, garlic and egg in a bowl. Mix well to combine, then divide into four equal portions and shape into patties just slightly larger than your buns. Use your thumb to make a small indentation in the centre of each patty, to help them retain their shape during cooking and prevent doming.

Heat the olive oil in a frying pan over medium–high heat. Season the patties well with salt and pepper and cook for 3–4 minutes, until well seared with a caramelised crust. Flip the patties over and cook for a further 2–3 minutes. Add a slice of cheese to each and fry for another minute, or until the cheese has melted and the patty is cooked to your liking.

Meanwhile, melt the butter in another frying pan over medium heat. Add the pastrami and toss for a minute or two, until warmed through. Leaving it in the pan, divide the pastrami into four even portions and top them with the remaining cheese slices. Turn the heat off and cover with a lid, allowing the cheese to melt over the warm pastrami.

To build your burgers, spread the cut sides of the buns with the butter and toast on a flat grill for a minute or two, until golden brown and buttery. Spread some dressing over the bun base and top with a beef patty, then some cheesy pastrami and the sauerkraut. Spread more dressing over the inside of the bun tops and place them on the burgers. Serve with crunchy dill pickles on the side.

PHILLY CHEESESTEAK

BEEF

45 g (1½ oz) salted butter

1 onion, sliced

1 red bell pepper (capsicum), sliced into strips

1 green bell pepper (capsicum), sliced into strips

sea salt and cracked black pepper

800 g (1 lb 12 oz) minced (ground) beef chuck (20% fat)

1½ tablespoons worcestershire sauce

1½ tablespoons olive oil

350 g (12 oz) ribeye steak, very finely sliced (see Note)

8 slices provolone cheese

TO SERVE

4 sesame seed hamburger buns, lightly toasted

60 g (2 oz) Garlic butter (page 20), melted

Crispy fried onion rings (page 37)

Melt 30 g (1 oz) of the butter in a frying pan over medium heat. Add the onion, peppers and a little salt and pepper and saute for about 7 minutes, until tender and cooked through. Remove from the pan and keep warm.

Meanwhile, place the beef chuck in a large bowl, add the worcestershire sauce and mix together. Divide into four equal portions and shape into patties just slightly larger than your buns. Use your thumb to make a small indentation in the centre of each patty, to help them retain their shape during cooking and prevent doming.

Warm 1 tablespoon of the olive oil in the pan you cooked the vegetables. Season the patties well with salt and pepper and cook for 3–4 minutes on one side, until seared and browned. Flip them over and cook the other side for a further 3 minutes, or until done to your liking. Remove and keep warm.

Add the remaining oil and butter to the pan. Add the ribeye slices, season with a little salt and pepper and cook for 3–4 minutes, until nicely seared.

Add the cooked onion and peppers to the pan, divide the mixture into four portions and top each portion with two slices of provolone. Turn off the heat, cover with a lid and leave for about 1 minute, until the cheese has just melted.

To build your burgers, brush your bun bases with the garlic butter. Add a beef patty to each and top with the cheesy steak, onion and pepper mixture. Finish with the bun tops and serve with a side of crispy onion rings.

NOTE

You'll find it easier to slice the ribeye steak into thin strips if you pop it in the freezer for about 20 minutes before slicing.

THE AUSSIE

BEEF

600 g (1 lb 5 oz) minced (ground) beef sirloin (20% fat)

sea salt and cracked black pepper

2 tablespoons olive oil

8 slices streaky bacon

4 free-range eggs

1 onion, sliced into 5 mm (¼ in) rings

TO SERVE

4 hamburger buns, lightly toasted and buttered

Mayonnaise (page 16)

handful of butter lettuce leaves

8 tomato slices, about 5 mm (¼ in) thick

8 tinned beetroot slices, drained

4 tinned pineapple rings, drained

barbecue sauce

Divide the beef into four equal portions and shape into patties just slightly larger than your buns. Use your thumb to make a small indentation in the centre of each patty, to help them retain their shape during cooking and prevent doming.

Season both sides of the patties well with salt and pepper.

Heat a cast-iron frying pan over medium–high heat. Add 1 tablespoon of the olive oil and cook the patties for 3–4 minutes on each side, until well seared with a caramelised crust, or until cooked to your liking.

While the patties are cooking, set up another large frying pan over medium heat. Add 2 teaspoons of the remaining olive oil and fry the bacon until crispy. Remove from the pan and keep warm.

Crack the eggs into the same pan and fry them in the bacon fat for a few minutes until cooked to your liking. Remove and keep warm. Add the final teaspoon of oil to the pan and fry the onion rings for a few minutes on each side until golden and charred.

To build your burgers, slather the base buns with mayonnaise, then pile on the lettuce, tomato, beetroot and a beef patty. Add the pineapple, onion, bacon, a fried egg and a generous drizzle of barbecue sauce, and finish with the bun tops.

BUFFALO CHICKEN

600 g (1 lb 5 oz) minced (ground) chicken

1 egg, beaten

50 g (½ cup) dried breadcrumbs

35 g (½ cup) crumbled blue cheese

2 garlic cloves, minced

1½ tablespoons hot sauce (such as Frank's)

1 teaspoon onion powder

½ teaspoon ground white pepper

1 tablespoon olive oil

sea salt and cracked black pepper

3C SLAW (CABBAGE, CARROT & CELERY SLAW)

115 g (1½ cups) finely sliced cabbage

2 celery stalks, finely sliced

1 small carrot, grated

¼ red onion, finely sliced

60–125 ml (¼–½ cup) blue cheese dressing or ranch dressing (to taste)

cracked black pepper, to taste

BUFFALO SAUCE

125 ml (½ cup) hot sauce (such as Frank's)

90 g (3 oz) butter, melted

TO SERVE

4 brioche buns, lightly toasted and buttered

blue cheese dressing or ranch dressing

dill pickles

carrot sticks

celery stalks

Place all the slaw ingredients in a large bowl and toss to combine.

Place the chicken in a bowl with the egg, breadcrumbs, cheese, garlic, hot sauce, onion powder and white pepper. Mix to combine, then divide into four equal portions and shape into patties just slightly larger than your buns. Use your thumb to make a small indentation in the centre of each patty, to help them retain their shape during cooking and prevent doming.

Heat the olive oil in a cast-iron frying pan over medium heat. Season the chicken patties with salt and black pepper and fry for about 4 minutes on each side, until golden brown and cooked through, and the internal temperature has reached 74°C (165°F).

Meanwhile, mix the buffalo sauce ingredients together in a bowl and keep warm.

Remove the cooked patties to a plate and generously spoon over some of the buffalo sauce, drenching them in the buttery sauce.

To build your burgers, pile the base buns with the slaw, then top with a chicken patty and a good spoonful of your chosen dressing. Finish with the bun tops. Serve with dill pickles, carrot sticks and celery stalks, with the remaining buffalo sauce and extra dressing on the side.

GOCHUJANG-GLAZED KFC

CHICKEN, TURKEY & DUCK

125 ml (½ cup) buttermilk

1 teaspoon rice wine vinegar

1 teaspoon finely grated ginger

¼ teaspoon sea salt

¼ teaspoon ground white pepper

4 boneless, skinless chicken thighs

peanut oil, for shallow-frying

SPICY GOCHUJANG SAUCE

2 tablespoons tamari

2 tablespoons honey

2 tablespoons brown sugar

1½ tablespoons gochujang paste

1½ tablespoons ketchup

2 teaspoons sesame oil

2 garlic cloves, minced

1 teaspoon finely grated ginger

KIMCHI CABBAGE SLAW

190 g (2½ cups) shredded red cabbage

75 g (½ cup) kimchi

60 g (¼ cup) Kewpie mayonnaise

1–2 teaspoons sriracha chilli sauce, to taste

1 teaspoon toasted sesame seeds

FLOUR DREDGE

60 g (½ cup) cornflour (corn starch)

35 g (¼ cup) plain (all-purpose) flour

½ teaspoon sea salt

TO SERVE

4 brioche buns, lightly toasted and buttered

Kewpie mayonnaise

Quick-pickled cucumber ribbons (page 34)

1 teaspoon toasted sesame seeds

½ teaspoon gochugaru red pepper flakes

In a shallow bowl, whisk together the buttermilk, vinegar, ginger, salt and pepper. Add the chicken and toss to coat, completely covering it in the buttermilk mixture. Cover and refrigerate for at least 2 hours, or up to 6 hours.

Meanwhile, place all the spicy gochujang sauce ingredients in a small saucepan and simmer over medium heat for a few minutes, whisking until the sugar has dissolved. Set aside for serving; the sauce will keep in a sealed glass jar in the fridge for 5–7 days.

When you're nearly ready to cook the chicken, toss all the kimchi cabbage slaw ingredients together in a large bowl and set aside.

Place the flour dredge ingredients in a shallow bowl and whisk to combine.

Remove the chicken from the marinade and dredge in the flour mixture, making sure the chicken is well coated. Set aside on a wire rack for about 15 minutes, to allow the flour coating to stick to the chicken.

Meanwhile, pour 7.5 cm (3 in) of peanut oil into a large deep frying pan or saucepan and heat to 180ºC (350ºF) over medium heat.

When your oil is hot, carefully cook the chicken in batches to avoid overcrowding the pan. Fry the chicken for about 12 minutes, turning a few times during cooking for even colouring. The chicken is done when it is golden brown, crispy and has an internal temperature of 74ºC (165ºF). Transfer to a wire rack lined with paper towel to absorb the excess oil.

When all the chicken pieces are cooked, place them in a bowl with the spicy gochujang sauce and toss until the chicken is completely coated.

To build your burgers, drizzle the base buns with mayonnaise, add some slaw, the spicy glazed chicken, a few pickled cucumber ribbons and a sprinkling of sesame seeds and gochugaru flakes. Drizzle a little more mayo on the inside of the bun tops to finish.

KATSU CHICKEN

2 boneless, skinless chicken breasts, sliced in half horizontally

2 eggs

150 g (1 cup) plain (all-purpose) flour

30 g (¼ cup) cornflour (corn starch)

¼ teaspoon ground white pepper

60 g (1 cup) panko breadcrumbs

1½ teaspoons togarashi seasoning (see Note)

vegetable oil, for shallow-frying

sea salt flakes

WOMBOK SLAW

2 teaspoons toasted sesame seed oil

4 teaspoons rice wine vinegar

1 teaspoon finely grated ginger

225 g (3 cups) shredded wombok (Chinese cabbage)

1 nashi pear, julienned

1 spring onion (scallion), finely sliced

1 teaspoon toasted sesame seeds

pinch of ground white pepper, to taste

TO SERVE

4 sesame seed hamburger buns, lightly toasted and buttered

Kewpie mayonnaise

tonkatsu sauce (Japanese barbecue sauce)

To make the wombok slaw, place the sesame oil, vinegar and ginger in a large mixing bowl and whisk to combine. Add the cabbage, pear, spring onion and sesame seeds, tossing well in the dressing. Taste and add a pinch of white pepper as desired.

Slightly flatten out the chicken pieces by lightly pounding them with a flat meat mallet or rolling pin. You want them to be of even thickness, so they cook quickly and evenly.

Set up a dredging station with three shallow bowls. In one bowl, whisk the eggs. In the second bowl, mix together the plain flour, cornflour and white pepper. In the third bowl, mix together the panko crumbs and togarashi.

Pour about 2.5 cm (1 in) of vegetable oil into a large deep frying pan and heat to 180°C (350°F) over medium heat.

While the oil is heating, dredge the chicken pieces, one at a time, in the egg, then the flour, then the egg again, before coating them completely in the panko crumbs.

When your oil is hot, carefully fry the chicken in batches for 3–4 minutes on each side, until the chicken is golden brown and has reached an internal temperature of 74°C (165°F).

Transfer the chicken to a wire rack lined with paper towel to absorb the excess oil. Sprinkle with salt flakes.

To build your burgers, slather the base buns with mayonnaise, then add a mound of wombok slaw and the chicken. Drizzle with more mayo and a good squiggle of tonkatsu sauce, then finish with the bun tops and enjoy.

NOTE

Togarashi is a popular Japanese seasoning mix containing dried red chilli and other spices. You'll find it in supermarkets and Asian grocers.

PULLED DUCK WITH PICKLED SLAW

 **CHICKEN, TURKEY & DUCK**

4 duck leg quarters, about 1 kg
(2 lb 3 oz) in total

6 garlic cloves, peeled

1 tablespoon sea salt, plus extra
for seasoning

125 ml (½ cup) barbecue sauce
or hoisin sauce

sea salt and cracked black pepper

TO SERVE

4 sesame seed milk buns, lightly
toasted and buttered

Kewpie mayonnaise

Pickled slaw (page 100)

sliced long red chilli

Pickled red onion (page 21) or sliced
fresh red onion

coriander (cilantro) sprigs (optional)

Preheat the oven to 170°C (340°F).

Use a skewer or sharp knife to pierce the skin on the duck legs, without piercing the flesh. This will help the skin to release the fat while cooking, ensuring a crispy skin. Pop the duck into a casserole dish (Dutch oven), add the garlic cloves and sprinkle with the 1 tablespoon of sea salt. Bake, uncovered, for about 2 hours, until the meat is tender and easily separates from the bone, and the skin is crispy. Remove from the oven and set aside until cool enough to handle.

Using a sharp knife, remove the crispy skin and reserve for serving. Pull the meat from the bones and shred into chunky pieces.

Transfer 2 tablespoons of the duck fat from the bottom of the casserole dish to a frying pan and place over medium heat. (Strain the remaining duck fat into a sterilised jar and store in the fridge for a future use, such as roasting potatoes.)

Add the shredded duck meat to the pan and stir through the barbecue or hoisin sauce until the meat is completely coated. Taste and season with salt and pepper as desired.

To build your burgers, drizzle some mayonnaise on the base buns, then add some slaw, saucy pulled duck, chilli slices, the reserved crispy duck skin, red onion and coriander sprigs, if using. Finish with the bun tops and enjoy.

CHICKEN PARMA

2 large boneless, skinless chicken breasts

75 g (½ cup) plain (all-purpose) flour

sea salt and cracked black pepper

2 eggs, beaten

90 g (1½ cups) panko breadcrumbs

2 teaspoons dried Italian herb seasoning

50 g (½ cup) grated parmesan

olive oil, for shallow-frying

310 g (1¼ cups) Napoli sauce (page 25) or store-bought napoletana pasta sauce

8 basil leaves

1 large ball of fresh mozzarella, sliced into 8 portions

TO SERVE

handful of rocket (arugula)

handful of radicchio leaves, torn

1 tablespoon lemon juice

1 tablespoon olive oil

4 ciabatta-style buns, or rosemary focaccia, lightly toasted and buttered

aioli

basil leaves

grated parmesan

Butterfly the chicken breasts, cutting all the way through, so that you have four pieces. Now cut each piece in half horizontally, so you have eight similar-sized chicken steaks. Place them in between two sheets of baking paper. Using a rolling pin or meat mallet, pound them out slightly, to an even thickness of about 1 cm (½ in).

Set up your crumbing station with three shallow bowls. Place the flour in one bowl and season with salt and pepper. Whisk the eggs in a second bowl. In the third bowl, mix together the panko crumbs, Italian seasoning and half the parmesan.

Dredge each piece of chicken through the flour, then the egg and finally the panko breadcrumb mixture, pressing on the crumbs to adhere to the chicken.

Pour about 2.5 cm (1 in) of olive oil into a cast-iron frying pan and heat over medium heat. When the oil is hot, fry the chicken in batches for 3–4 minutes on each side, until the chicken is golden brown and cooked through and has reached an internal temperature of 74°C (165°F).

Meanwhile, preheat the grill (broiler) to medium–high.

Place the fried chicken on a baking tray lined with baking paper. Dollop some napoli sauce on each piece of chicken, then top with a basil leaf, the remaining parmesan and a piece of mozzarella. Pop under the grill for a minute or two, until the cheese has melted.

Meanwhile, place the rocket, radicchio, lemon juice and olive oil in a bowl and toss to combine.

To build your burgers, slather the inside of the base buns and bun tops with aioli. Add some salad leaves to the bottom buns, then top each with two slices of chicken, a few basil leaves and some more grated parmesan. Finish with the bun tops and enjoy.

SOUTHERN FRIED CHICKEN WAFFLE

CHICKEN, TURKEY & DUCK

4 boneless, skinless chicken thighs

250 ml (1 cup) buttermilk

1 tablespoon hot sauce (such as Frank's)

100 g (⅔ cup) plain (all-purpose) flour

40 g (⅓ cup) cornflour (corn starch)

1½ teaspoons cracked black pepper

1½ teaspoons onion powder

1½ teaspoons smoked paprika

1½ teaspoons garlic powder

1 teaspoon cayenne pepper

1 teaspoon sea salt

¼ teaspoon celery salt

peanut oil, for deep-frying

sea salt flakes

SWEET 'N' SPICY HOT SYRUP

60 g (2 oz) butter

2½ tablespoons maple syrup

1 teaspoon sweet paprika

½ teaspoon chilli flakes, or to taste

½ teaspoon chilli powder, or to taste

½ teaspoon sea salt

¼–½ teaspoon cayenne pepper (see Note)

¼ teaspoon cracked black pepper

TO SERVE

8 waffles, warmed and buttered

sliced dill pickles

8 slices crispy bacon

4 fried eggs

1 tablespoon finely chopped chives

For very tender chicken, start this recipe the day before. Place the chicken, buttermilk and hot sauce in a shallow bowl and toss to coat. Cover and leave to marinate in the fridge overnight.

When ready to cook, place all the sweet 'n' spicy hot syrup ingredients in a small saucepan and stir over medium–low heat until the butter has melted and all the ingredients have combined. Keep warm for serving; the syrup will keep in a sealed glass jar in the fridge for up to 2 weeks.

Place the plain flour, cornflour and all the spices and salts in a shallow bowl and whisk to combine.

Remove the chicken from the buttermilk and discard the liquid. Dredge the chicken through the flour mixture, then place on a wire rack.

Meanwhile, pour about 7.5 cm (3 in) of peanut oil into a large deep frying pan or saucepan and heat to 180°C (350°F) over medium heat.

When the oil is hot, carefully place the chicken pieces, one at a time, into the pan and fry for 4–5 minutes on each side, until golden brown and cooked through. The chicken is ready when it has reached an internal temperature of 74ºC (165ºF). Transfer to a wire rack lined with paper towel to absorb the excess oil. Sprinkle with salt flakes.

When you are ready to build your burgers, drench the fried chicken pieces with the sweet 'n' spicy hot syrup.

Use four of the waffles as the base buns, topping them with pickle slices, the syrup-drenched chicken, two crispy bacon slices and a fried egg. Sprinkle with the chives, then top with the remaining waffles. Serve with the remaining sweet 'n' spicy hot syrup on the side.

NOTE

The sweet 'n' spicy hot syrup has a little kick, so start with half the amount of cayenne pepper, then add more as desired.

THE CDMX

CHICKEN, TURKEY & DUCK

4 boneless chicken thighs, skin on

1 tablespoon olive oil

TEQUILA MARINADE

2 tablespoons olive oil

2 tablespoons tequila

2 tablespoons brown sugar

zest and juice of 2 limes

3 tablespoons chopped coriander (cilantro) leaves

2–3 garlic cloves, minced

1 teaspoon chilli powder

1 teaspoon salt

½ teaspoon ground cumin

½ teaspoon onion powder

½ teaspoon black pepper

TO SERVE

4 brioche buns, toasted and buttered

Lime paprika crema (page 30)

225 g (3 cups) finely shredded red cabbage

coriander (cilantro) sprigs

Tomatillo salsa verde (page 31)

1 avocado, sliced

Pickled red onion (page 21)

Place all the tequila marinade ingredients in a large glass or ceramic bowl and whisk to combine. Add the chicken thighs and toss to coat well, then cover and marinate in the fridge for 3–4 hours.

Remove the chicken from the marinade, discarding the liquid. Heat a cast-iron frying pan or grill pan over medium–high heat and brush with the olive oil. Cook the chicken for 4–5 minutes on each side, until the chicken is cooked through and has reached an internal temperature of 74°C (165°F).

To build your burgers, slather the base buns with lime paprika crema, then top with the cabbage and coriander. Drizzle with a little more crema and add the chicken, salsa verde, avocado and pickled onion. Finish with the bun tops and enjoy.

PERI PERI CHICKEN

4 boneless, skinless chicken thighs

1 tablespoon olive oil

4 slices American-style cheese (optional)

PERI PERI SAUCE

2 roasted or marinated red bell peppers (capsicums) in oil, chopped

3 garlic cloves, peeled

2–3 small red chillies, seeds removed (unless you like it really hot)

60 ml (¼ cup) olive oil

2 tablespoons lemon juice

2 tablespoons red wine vinegar

2 teaspoons chopped oregano leaves

1 teaspoon smoked paprika

1 teaspoon sweet paprika

1 teaspoon sea salt

1 teaspoon chilli flakes

¼ teaspoon cracked black pepper

TO SERVE

4 brioche buns, lightly toasted and buttered

Mayonnaise (page 16)

Rainbow slaw (page 28)

Place all the peri peri sauce ingredients in a food processor and blitz to combine.

Pour 125 ml (½ cup) of the peri peri sauce into a bowl, add the chicken and toss well. Cover and allow to marinate in the fridge for 2–4 hours, or overnight. Meanwhile, refrigerate the remaining sauce until ready to serve; it will keep in a sealed glass jar for up to 5 days.

When ready to cook, heat the olive oil in a large frying pan over medium heat. Cook the marinated chicken thighs for 4–5 minutes on each side, until the chicken is well browned and has reached an internal temperature of 74°C (165°F). During the final minute of cooking, top with the cheese slices, if using, and allow to melt.

To build your burgers, slather the base buns with mayonnaise, then add some slaw and the chicken. Drizzle with the reserved peri peri sauce and finish with the bun tops.

MY BIG FAT GREEK CHICKEN

CHICKEN, TURKEY & DUCK

1 tablespoon olive oil

½ lemon

LEMON YOGHURT SAUCE

250 g (1 cup) Greek-style yoghurt

2 tablespoons lemon juice

1 tablespoon finely chopped mint leaves

1 garlic clove, minced

¼ teaspoon ground cumin

good pinch of sea salt

good pinch of cracked black pepper

CHICKEN PATTIES

600 g (1 lb 5 oz) minced (ground) chicken

80 g (2¾ oz) feta, crumbled

1 large egg

15 g (¼ cup) panko breadcrumbs

½ red onion, very finely diced

3 garlic cloves, minced

1 tablespoon finely chopped dill fronds

2 teaspoons finely chopped oregano

zest of ½ small lemon

½ teaspoon sea salt flakes

½ teaspoon cracked black pepper

SPINACH, ROCKET & CUCUMBER SALAD

2 handfuls of baby spinach

handful of rocket (arugula)

1 short cucumber, finely sliced into ribbons

¼ cup dill sprigs

TO SERVE

4 Turkish buns, toasted and buttered

4 thick heirloom tomato slices

finely sliced red onion

creamy marinated Persian feta

kalamata olives

Place all the lemon yoghurt sauce ingredients in a bowl and whisk to combine. Taste, then add a little more seasoning as desired. The sauce will keep in an airtight container in the fridge for up to 5 days.

In a large bowl, gently mix together all the patty ingredients. Divide into four equal portions, then shape into patties slightly bigger than your buns. Use your thumb to make a small indentation in the centre of each patty, to help them retain their shape during cooking and prevent doming.

Heat a large cast-iron frying pan over medium heat and add the olive oil. When hot, cook the patties for 4–5 minutes on each side, until they are golden brown and have reached an internal temperature of 74°C (165°F). Transfer the patties to a plate and squeeze the lemon juice over. Cover and keep warm for 2–3 minutes.

While the patties are resting, place all the salad ingredients in a mixing bowl, drizzle on as much lemon yoghurt sauce as you'd like, then toss to combine.

To build your burgers, spoon a little lemon yoghurt sauce on the base buns. Add the spinach salad, tomato slices, chicken patties, red onion and dollops of creamy feta. Finish with the bun tops, then skewer a few olives onto four toothpicks and push them through your burgers to hold them all together.

TEX MEX TURKEY

600 g (1 lb 5 oz) minced (ground) turkey

25 g (¼ cup) dried breadcrumbs

¼ cup chopped coriander (cilantro) leaves

2 spring onions (scallions), finely sliced

2 garlic cloves, minced

1 chipotle chilli in adobo sauce, finely chopped, plus 1 tablespoon of the adobo sauce

1 teaspoon ground cumin

½ teaspoon sea salt

¼ teaspoon cracked black pepper

1 tablespoon olive oil

4 slices pepper jack or monterey jack cheese

TO SERVE

4 brioche buns, lightly toasted and buttered

Chipotle crema (page 30)

butter lettuce leaves

guacamole

Pico de gallo salsa (page 31)

sliced pickled jalapeno chillies

Place the turkey in a bowl with the breadcrumbs, coriander, spring onion, garlic, chipotle chilli, adobo sauce, cumin, salt and pepper. Mix together, then divide into four equal portions and shape into patties just slightly bigger than your buns. Use your thumb to make a small indentation in the centre of each patty, to help them retain their shape during cooking and prevent doming. Cover and refrigerate for 20–30 minutes.

To cook the patties, place a cast-iron frying pan over medium heat and add the olive oil. Fry the patties for 4–5 minutes on each side, until they are cooked through and have reached an internal temperature of 74°C (165°F). During the final minute of cooking, top with the cheese slices and cover with a lid to melt the cheese.

To build your burgers, slather the base buns with chipotle crema and top with lettuce leaves. Add the turkey patties, guacamole and salsa and finish with the bun tops. Serve with sliced pickled jalapeno chillies on the side.

THE BIG BREAKFAST

PORK AND LAMB

600 g (1 lb 5 oz) minced (ground) pork

1½ teaspoons brown sugar

1 teaspoon chopped sage leaves

1 teaspoon thyme leaves

1 teaspoon onion powder

½ teaspoon cracked black pepper

good pinch of cayenne pepper

1 teaspoon sea salt

1 tablespoon olive oil

4 slices American-style cheese

TO SERVE

4 English muffins or brioche buns, lightly toasted and buttered

dijonnaise

2 handfuls of baby spinach

4 store-bought hash browns, cooked

tomato chutney or ketchup

8 slices crispy smoked bacon

4 fried eggs

cracked black pepper

Tabasco sauce (optional)

To make the burger patties, place the pork in a mixing bowl with the sugar, herbs, spices and salt. Mix together well, then divide into four equal portions and shape into patties slightly bigger than your muffins or buns. Use your thumb to make a small indentation in the centre of each patty, to help them retain their shape during cooking and prevent doming.

Heat a cast-iron frying pan over medium heat and add the olive oil. When hot, fry the patties for 2–3 minutes on each side, until they are cooked through and reach an internal temperature of 71°C (160°F). For the final minute of cooking, add a slice of cheese to each patty.

To build your burgers, slather the base muffins or buns with dijonnaise, then add some baby spinach, a hash brown, tomato chutney or ketchup and a pork patty. Top each with two crispy bacon slices, a fried egg, a crack of black pepper and a good splash of Tabasco sauce, if using. Slather more dijonnaise on the muffin or bun tops, place them on the burgers and enjoy.

SPICY LAMB WITH TZATZIKI

PORK AND LAMB

600 g (1 lb 5 oz) minced (ground) lamb (20% fat)

5 teaspoons harissa paste

5 teaspoons toasted pine nuts

5 teaspoons finely chopped parsley

60 g (2 oz) Greek-style feta, crumbled

1 teaspoon cracked black pepper

sea salt

1 tablespoon olive oil

TO SERVE

4 hamburger buns, lightly toasted and buttered

Tzatziki (page 24)

2 handfuls of watercress

½ cup mint leaves

½ cup coriander (cilantro) leaves

2 roasted red bell peppers (capsicums) in oil, sliced

creamy marinated Persian feta

Place the lamb in a large bowl with the harissa paste, pine nuts, parsley, feta and black pepper and mix to combine. Divide into four equal portions and gently shape into patties slightly bigger than your buns. Cover and chill in the fridge for 20–30 minutes.

Season the burgers with a good sprinkling of sea salt. Heat the olive oil in a cast-iron frying pan over medium–high heat. Cook the burgers for 3–4 minutes on each side, until well browned and cooked to your liking (an internal temperature of 65–70°C/149–158°F is medium). Remove from the heat, cover and leave to rest for about 2 minutes.

To build your burgers, slather the base buns with tzatziki, then layer with the watercress, herbs and a lamb burger. Top with the roasted red peppers and chunks of creamy feta. Add an extra dollop of tzatziki, finish with the bun tops and enjoy.

THE CUBANO

600 g (1 lb 5 oz) minced (ground) pork

1 garlic clove, minced

2 teaspoons chopped oregano leaves

1 teaspoon ground cumin

1 teaspoon worcestershire sauce

½ teaspoon cayenne pepper (optional)

sea salt and cracked black pepper

1 tablespoon olive oil

4 slices Swiss cheese

TO SERVE

4 sesame seed hamburger buns, lightly toasted and spread with Garlic butter (page 20)

American mustard

sliced dill pickles

120 g (4½ oz) shaved smoked ham

Mayonnaise (page 16)

Place the pork in a large mixing bowl with the garlic, oregano, cumin and worcestershire sauce. Add the cayenne pepper, if using, and season with sea salt and cracked black pepper. Combine well, taking care not to overwork the mixture. Divide into four equal portions and shape into patties slightly larger than your buns. Use your thumb to make a small indentation in the centre of each patty, to help them retain their shape during cooking and prevent doming.

Heat a cast-iron frying pan over medium–high heat and add the olive oil. When the oil is hot, cook the burgers for 3–4 minutes on each side, until cooked through and golden brown with a crisp crust, and with an internal temperature of 71°C (160°F). For the final minute of cooking, place a cheese slice on each patty, cover with a lid and allow to melt.

To build your burgers, slather the base buns with mustard, then add the pork patties, sliced dill pickles and shaved ham. Slather a little mayonnaise and more mustard on the inside of the bun tops, place them on the burgers and enjoy.

CLASSIC PULLED PORK

1.5 kg (3 lb 5 oz) pork shoulder (weight without skin and fat cap)

250 ml (1 cup) cloudy apple juice

60 ml (¼ cup) apple cider vinegar, plus extra (optional)

1 tablespoon dijon mustard

1 tablespoon worcestershire sauce

125–185 ml (½–¾ cup) barbecue sauce

sea salt and cracked black pepper

SPICE RUB

1 tablespoon smoked paprika

1 tablespoon brown sugar

2 teaspoons sea salt flakes

1 teaspoon chilli flakes

1 teaspoon onion powder

1 teaspoon garlic powder

½–1 teaspoon cayenne pepper, to taste

1 teaspoon cracked black pepper

TO SERVE

4 sesame seed hamburger buns, lightly toasted and buttered

Creamy coleslaw (page 28)

sliced dill pickles

Preheat the oven to 160°C (320°F).

Combine all the spice rub ingredients in a small bowl.

Cut the pork shoulder into three or four large even pieces and place in a large ovenproof casserole dish (Dutch oven). Sprinkle over the spice rub and massage it into the pork to coat all over.

Add the apple juice, vinegar, mustard and worcestershire sauce, then cover and pop into the oven to cook low and slow for 3 hours.

Remove the lid and cook the pork for a further 30 minutes or until the meat is very tender and easily shreds when pulled apart with two forks. Shred all the pork.

Place the shredded pork in a frying pan or saucepan over low heat and mix in enough barbecue sauce to thoroughly coat it, adding more sauce as desired. Warm the mixture, then season with salt, pepper or more apple cider vinegar to your liking.

Pile the pulled pork onto the base buns, then top with plenty of coleslaw and sliced dill pickles. Finish with the bun tops.

CHORIZO WITH PAPRIKA AIOLI

PORK AND LAMB

500 g (1 lb 2 oz) fresh chorizo sausages, casings removed

100 g (3½ oz) minced (ground) lean beef

¼ cup chopped parsley leaves

1 teaspoon olive oil

sea salt and cracked black pepper

4 slices manchego cheese (or cheddar)

PAPRIKA AIOLI

125 g (½ cup) Mayonnaise (page 16)

2 teaspoons Spanish sherry vinegar

1 garlic clove, minced

½ teaspoon smoked paprika

½ teaspoon sweet paprika

pinch of cayenne pepper

pinch of sea salt

TO SERVE

4 hamburger buns, lightly toasted and buttered

romesco sauce (store bought)

2 handfuls of rocket (arugula)

Grilled onion (page 21)

Place the paprika aioli ingredients in a bowl and whisk to combine. Taste, and adjust the seasoning as desired. The aioli will keep in a sealed glass jar in the fridge for up to 1 week.

To make the burgers, crumble the chorizo into a large bowl, add the beef and parsley and mix to combine. Divide the mixture into four equal portions and shape into patties just slightly larger than your buns.

Place a cast-iron frying pan over medium heat and add the olive oil. Season the patties well on each side with salt and pepper, then cook for about 4 minutes on each side, until well seared and browned, and with an internal temperature of 71°C (160°F). For the final minute of cooking, place a cheese slice on each patty and allow to melt. Remove from the heat and leave to rest for a minute or two.

To build your burgers, slather the base buns with romesco sauce, then add the rocket, patties and grilled onion. Dollop some paprika aioli on the inside of the bun tops, place them on the burgers and enjoy.

ITALIAN PORK SAUSAGE <u>WITH</u> BURRATA & PISTACHIO PESTO

80 g (1 cup) fresh white breadcrumbs

60 ml (¼ cup) milk

600 g (1 lb 5 oz) Italian fennel and chilli pork sausages, casings removed

1 egg

2 tablespoons finely chopped parsley

2 teaspoons olive oil

PISTACHIO PESTO

65 g (½ cup) chopped pistachios

80 g (2¾ oz) basil leaves

2 garlic cloves, peeled

45 g (½ cup) grated pecorino

125 ml (½ cup) extra virgin olive oil, plus extra to make the pesto a drizzling consistency

sea salt and cracked black pepper

TO SERVE

4 ciabatta buns, lightly toasted and buttered

Mayonnaise (page 16)

2 large handfuls of rocket (arugula)

200 g (7 oz) sliced mortadella

200 g (7 oz) burrata, torn

pickled Italian cherry peppers

Place all the pistachio pesto ingredients in a food processor and blitz to combine. Taste and season with salt and pepper as desired. Drizzle with extra olive oil to make the pesto a drizzling consistency. The pesto will keep in a sealed glass jar in the fridge for 6–7 days.

To make the patties, place the breadcrumbs and milk in a bowl and leave to soak for a few minutes. Squeeze the excess milk from the bread and discard the milk, then place the bread in a fresh bowl with the sausage meat, egg and parsley. Mix to combine, then divide into four equal portions and shape into patties. Use your thumb to make a small indentation in the centre of each patty, to help them retain their shape during cooking and prevent doming.

Heat a cast-iron frying pan over medium–high heat and add the olive oil. When hot, cook the patties for about 4 minutes on each side, until they are nicely browned and have an internal temperature of 72ºC (162ºF).

To build your burgers, slather the base buns with mayonnaise and add the rocket. Top each with a pork sausage patty, the mortadella, burrata and a good drizzle of pistachio pesto. Finish with the bun tops and serve with pickled Italian cherry peppers on the side.

HAWAIIAN TERIYAKI PORK WITH GRILLED PINEAPPLE

500 g (1 lb 2 oz) minced (ground) pork

30 g (½ cup) panko breadcrumbs

2–3 garlic cloves, minced

1 large spring onion (scallion), finely sliced

2 teaspoons finely grated ginger

1 egg, beaten

sea salt and cracked black pepper

2 teaspoons olive oil

4 pineapple rings

1 onion, sliced into rings

2 teaspoons toasted sesame oil

TERIYAKI SAUCE

60 ml (¼ cup) mirin

60 ml (¼ cup) soy sauce

60 ml (¼ cup) sake

55 g (¼ cup) firmly packed brown sugar

1 tablespoon honey

½ teaspoon finely grated ginger

2 teaspoons cornflour (corn starch)

TO SERVE

4 sesame seed hamburger buns, lightly toasted and buttered

Kewpie mayonnaise

mixed salad leaves

To make the teriyaki sauce, place the mirin, soy sauce, sake, sugar, honey and ginger in a small saucepan. Bring to the boil over medium–high heat, then reduce the heat and simmer for about 10 minutes. Combine 2 tablespoons of water and the cornflour and whisk until smooth, then add to the teriyaki sauce and whisk until combined. Simmer for a further 3–4 minutes, whisking occasionally. Remove from the heat and set aside; the sauce will thicken slightly as it cools.

Place the pork in a large bowl with the breadcrumbs, garlic, spring onion, ginger, egg and 4 teaspoons of the teriyaki sauce. Season with salt and pepper and mix to combine. Divide into four equal portions and shape into patties slightly larger than your buns. Use your thumb to make a small indentation in the centre of each patty, to help them retain their shape during cooking and prevent doming.

Heat a cast-iron frying pan or chargrill pan over medium–high heat and add the olive oil. When the oil is hot, cook the burgers for about 4 minutes on each side, until cooked through and with an internal temperature of 71°C (160°F).

While the burgers are cooking, heat a separate frying pan or chargrill pan over medium–high heat. Place the pineapple rings and onion rings in a bowl and toss through the sesame oil to coat. Cook the pineapple and onion for 3–4 minutes on each side until lightly charred. Set aside and keep warm.

Place the cooked patties in a wide shallow bowl and generously spoon the teriyaki sauce over, coating them well.

To build your burgers, slather the base buns with mayonnaise, then add the salad leaves, patties, grilled onion and grilled pineapple. Finish with a drizzle of teriyaki sauce, then add the bun tops and enjoy.

ITALIAN PORK MEATBALL SLIDERS

50 g (⅓ cup) plain (all-purpose) flour

3 tablespoons olive oil

1 x quantity Napoli sauce (page 25)

MEATBALLS

600 g (1 lb 5 oz) minced (ground) pork

1 small onion, grated

1 egg, beaten

25 g (¼ cup) dried breadcrumbs

35 g (⅓ cup) finely grated parmesan

2 garlic cloves, minced

3 tablespoons finely chopped parsley

¼ teaspoon chilli flakes

sea salt and cracked black pepper

TO SERVE

12 slider buns, lightly toasted

90 g (3 oz) Garlic butter (page 20), melted

3 slices provolone cheese, cut into quarters

grated parmesan

12 stuffed green olives

12 pickled peperoncino chillies

Place the meatball ingredients in a large mixing bowl, season well with salt and pepper and mix to combine. Using wet hands, evenly shape the mixture into 12 meatballs. Roll the meatballs in the flour to lightly coat.

Heat the olive oil in a cast-iron frying pan over medium–high heat. Working in two batches, cook the meatballs for 5–7 minutes, turning often, until evenly browned.

Preheat the oven to 160°C (320°F).

Meanwhile, return all the meatballs to the pan, add the napoli sauce and simmer for about 15 minutes, until the meatballs are fully cooked through.

To build your burgers, slather the base buns with the garlic butter. Top each with a saucy meatball, a piece of provolone and some grated parmesan, then transfer to the oven for 5 minutes to melt the cheese.

Remove the sliders from the oven and add the bun tops. Thread the olives and pepperoncino chillies onto small skewers and insert them into the top of the sliders. Serve with the remaining napoli sauce on the side for dipping.

ASIAN-STYLE DOUBLE PORK SCHNITZEL

PORK AND LAMB

8 boneless pork loin chops, about 600 g (1 lb 5 oz) in total, pounded to a 5 mm (¼ in) thickness

1½ teaspoons shichimi togarashi (see Note)

sea salt and cracked black pepper

75 g (½ cup) plain (all-purpose) flour

2 eggs

90 g (1½ cups) panko breadcrumbs

peanut oil, for shallow-frying

sea salt flakes

PICKLED SLAW

125 ml (½ cup) rice wine vinegar

115 g (½ cup) caster (superfine) sugar

1 teaspoon sea salt

150 g (2 cups) shredded red cabbage

2 radishes, finely sliced

1 carrot, finely shredded

½ small red onion, finely sliced

1 small red chilli, finely sliced

TO SERVE

4 sesame seed hamburger buns, lightly toasted and buttered

sriracha mayonnaise

1 short cucumber, finely sliced into ribbons

coriander (cilantro) sprigs

To prepare the pickled slaw, combine the vinegar, sugar and salt in a small saucepan and whisk over medium heat until the sugar has dissolved. Allow to cool. Place all the vegetables in a mixing bowl, then pour the pickling liquid over and toss to coat. Cover and refrigerate for 30–40 minutes before using; the slaw will keep in an airtight container in the fridge for up to 2 days.

When you're ready to cook, season the pork with the shichimi togarashi, salt and pepper.

Set up your crumbing station with three shallow bowls. Place the flour in one bowl, whisk the eggs in a second bowl and place the panko crumbs in the third bowl. Dredge the pork in the flour, shaking off the excess. Dip into the egg, coating evenly, then into the breadcrumbs, pressing them on to adhere and cover the pork completely.

Pour about 3 cm (1¼ in) of peanut oil into a cast-iron frying pan and heat to 180ºC (350ºF) over medium heat. Fry the pork in batches for 2–3 minutes on each side, until the pork is golden brown and cooked through, with an internal temperature of 68ºC (154ºF). Transfer to a wire rack lined with paper towel to absorb the excess oil. Sprinkle with salt flakes.

To build your burgers, slather the base buns with sriracha mayonnaise, then top each with some pickled slaw and two pork schnitzels. Add the cucumber and coriander, then slather more mayo on the inside of the bun tops. Place them on the burgers and enjoy.

NOTE

Also known as Japanese seven-spice, shichimi togarashi is a popular Japanese seasoning mix typically containing dried red chilli and other ingredients such as sansho pepper, dried orange peel, ginger, black and white sesame seeds, and nori flakes. You'll find it in supermarkets and Asian grocers.

LAMB KOFTAS <u>WITH</u> ALEPPO PEPPER MAYO

PORK AND LAMB

500 g (1 lb 2 oz) minced (ground) lamb (20% fat)

½ onion, grated or very finely chopped

4 teaspoons finely chopped parsley

2 teaspoons finely chopped mint leaves

4 garlic cloves, minced

1 tablespoon tomato puree (concentrated puree)

½ teaspoon ground cinnamon

½ teaspoon ground allspice

½ teaspoon ground cumin

½ teaspoon ground coriander

½ teaspoon hot paprika

½ teaspoon cracked black pepper

sea salt

1 tablespoon olive oil

ALEPPO PEPPER MAYONNAISE

125 g (½ cup) Mayonnaise (page 16)

1–1½ teaspoons Aleppo pepper, to taste

squeeze of lemon juice

sea salt

TO SERVE

4 sesame seed Turkish bread rolls, lightly toasted and buttered

2 handfuls of rocket (arugula)

1¼ cups mint leaves

1¼ cups parsley leaves

Tahini garlic yoghurt sauce (page 17)

8 juicy tomato slices

Turkish pickled vegetables (store bought)

Place the Aleppo pepper mayonnaise ingredients in a mixing bowl and whisk to combine. Taste and add a pinch of salt or more Aleppo pepper as desired. The mayo will keep in a sealed glass jar in the fridge for 5–7 days.

Place the lamb in a large bowl with the onion, parsley, mint, garlic and tomato puree. Add the spices, season with sea salt and gently mix to combine. Divide the mixture into four equal portions and shape into patties slightly bigger than your Turkish rolls. Use your thumb to make a small indentation in the centre of each patty, to help them retain their shape during cooking and prevent doming.

Heat the olive oil in a large cast-iron frying pan over medium heat. Fry the burgers for about 4 minutes on each side, until seared, well browned and cooked to your liking, or an internal temperature of 65°C (149°F) is reached for medium.

To build your burgers, slather the base rolls with the Aleppo pepper mayonnaise. Add the rocket, herbs and a lamb kofta burger. Top with a generous drizzle of tahini garlic yoghurt sauce and the tomato slices. Finish with the roll tops and serve with some Turkish pickled vegetables on the side.

NOTE

Aleppo pepper is a moderately spicy chilli pepper with a complex fruity, tangy flavour that is popular in Middle Eastern cuisine.

GRILLED PRAWN COCKTAIL SLIDERS

SEAFOOD

18 large raw prawns (shrimp), peeled and deveined

2 tablespoons olive oil

1 teaspoon lemon zest

2 teaspoons lemon juice

1 garlic clove, minced

¼ teaspoon sweet paprika

COCKTAIL SAUCE

125 g (½ cup) Mayonnaise (page 16)

3 tablespoons ketchup

1–2 teaspoons horseradish (optional)

1 teaspoon lemon juice

1 teaspoon Tabasco sauce

½ teaspoon worcestershire sauce

pinch of cayenne pepper

TO SERVE

6 brioche slider buns, lightly toasted and buttered

2 large handfuls of shredded iceberg lettuce

1 avocado, sliced

sea salt flakes

dill fronds

chopped chives

Place all the cocktail sauce ingredients in a bowl and whisk to combine. Cover and chill in the fridge until ready to use; the sauce will keep in an airtight container in the fridge for 5–7 days.

Toss the prawns in a bowl with the olive oil, lemon zest, lemon juice, garlic and paprika.

Heat a barbecue grill or cast-iron frying pan to medium–high. Add the prawns and grill for 2–3 minutes, turning with tongs as they cook.

To build your burgers, layer the base buns with the cocktail sauce, shredded lettuce and avocado slices. Sprinkle the avocado slices with salt flakes and add the prawns and herbs. Drizzle with more cocktail sauce and finish with the bun tops.

CALAMARI WITH LEMON CAPER AIOLI

SEAFOOD

360 g (12½ oz) small calamari tubes

250 ml (1 cup) buttermilk

150 g (1 cup) plain (all-purpose) flour

1½ teaspoons sea salt

1½ teaspoons cracked black pepper

1 teaspoon cayenne pepper

2 eggs

80 g (1⅓ cups) panko breadcrumbs

peanut oil, for deep-frying

sea salt flakes

LEMON CAPER AIOLI

125 g (½ cup) Mayonnaise (page 16)

2 garlic cloves, finely grated

2 teaspoons baby capers, rinsed

2 teaspoons lemon juice, plus extra (optional)

2 teaspoons chopped chives

1 teaspoon lemon zest

1 teaspoon dijon mustard

pinch of sea salt and cracked black pepper

TO SERVE

4 brioche buns or milk buns, lightly toasted and buttered

3 handfuls of shredded iceberg lettuce

Quick-pickled cucumber ribbons (page 34)

¼ cup chopped dill fronds

¼ cup chopped chives

lemon wedges

For the most tender calamari, start this recipe the night before. Place the calamari in a shallow glass or ceramic dish, pour in the buttermilk and turn to coat. Cover and marinate in the fridge overnight, to allow the buttermilk to tenderise the calamari.

In a small bowl, mix together the lemon caper aioli ingredients and set aside. Taste and add more lemon juice, if desired. The aioli will keep in a sealed glass jar in the fridge for up to 5 days.

To cook the calamari, set up three shallow bowls for dredging. In the first bowl, combine the flour, salt, pepper and cayenne pepper. Whisk the eggs in the second bowl, and spread the panko crumbs in the third dish.

Remove the calamari tubes from the buttermilk and slice into 1 cm (½ in) thick rings. Discard the buttermilk.

Pour about 7.5 cm (3 in) of peanut oil into a large deep frying pan or saucepan and heat to 180°C (350°F) over medium heat.

Dredge a few calamari rings at a time through the flour, then the egg, and finally the breadcrumbs, coating thoroughly. Set aside on a tray.

Carefully lower a few calamari rings, one at a time, into the hot oil, taking care to not overcrowd the pan. Cook for about 2 minutes, until golden brown. Transfer to a wire rack lined with paper towel to absorb the excess oil. Sprinkle with salt flakes.

To build your burgers, slather the base buns with the lemon caper aioli, then add the lettuce, cucumber ribbons, fried calamari and herbs. Smear a little more aioli on the inside of the bun tops and place them on the burgers. Serve with lemon wedges.

'FILET-O-FISH'

SEAFOOD

75 g (½ cup) plain (all-purpose) flour

2 eggs

1 tablespoon Mayonnaise (page 16)

1 tablespoon dijon mustard

1 teaspoon sweet paprika

90 g (1½ cups) panko breadcrumbs

500–600 g (1 lb 2–1 lb 5 oz) firm white fish fillet, such as rockling, cod or halibut, cut into 4 equal portions to fit your buns

sea salt and cracked black pepper

peanut oil, for shallow-frying

4 slices American-style cheese

TO SERVE

4 brioche hamburger buns, lightly toasted and buttered

Mayonnaise (page 16)

3 handfuls of shredded iceberg lettuce (optional)

¼ cup dill fronds (optional)

Tartar sauce (page 17)

cornichons

lemon wedges

Set up three shallow bowls for dredging the fish. Place the flour in the first bowl. In the second bowl, whisk together the eggs, mayonnaise, mustard and paprika. Spread the panko crumbs in the third bowl.

Season both sides of the fish fillets with salt and pepper, then dredge them through the flour, one at a time, shaking off any excess. Dredge the fillets through the egg mixture, then finally the breadcrumbs, coating thoroughly and pressing the crumbs on so they adhere.

Pour about 3 cm (1¼ in) of peanut oil into a large deep frying pan or saucepan and heat to 180ºC (350ºF) over medium heat.

Working in batches, carefully lower the fish fillets into the oil and fry for 2–2½ minutes on each side, until golden, crispy and cooked through. Transfer to a wire rack lined with paper towel to absorb the excess oil. Sprinkle with salt flakes and immediately place a slice of cheese on each piece of fish.

To build your burgers, slather the base buns with mayonnaise, then add the lettuce and dill, if using. Add a piece of fried fish to each burger, a good dollop of tartar sauce, and finish with the bun tops. Serve with cornichons and lemon wedges.

TURKISH MACKEREL WITH CHILLI & POMEGRANATE DRESSING

SEAFOOD

2 tablespoons olive oil

4 mackerel fillets, skin on, deboned

sea salt

CHILLI & POMEGRANATE DRESSING

2 tablespoons extra virgin olive oil

35 ml (1¼ fl oz) lemon juice

1 small garlic clove, finely grated

1 tablespoon pomegranate molasses

1 teaspoon ground sumac

1 teaspoon Aleppo pepper (see Notes)

¼ teaspoon Maras biber chilli flakes (see Notes)

¼ teaspoon Urfa biber chilli flakes (see Notes)

sea salt and cracked black pepper, to taste

TURKISH-STYLE SALAD

3 handfuls of shredded iceberg lettuce

2 tomatoes, diced

1 short cucumber, finely sliced into ribbons

¼ red onion, sliced

1 cup mixed mint, parsley and coriander (cilantro) leaves

TO SERVE

4 long Turkish rolls, toasted

Lemon yoghurt sauce (page 79)

lemon wedges

Place the chilli and pomegranate dressing ingredients in a glass jar and seal, then shake to combine. Taste and adjust the seasoning as desired. Reserve 1½ tablespoons of the dressing for basting the fish.

Place the Turkish-style salad ingredients in a bowl, pour over the remaining dressing and toss to combine.

Heat a barbecue grill or cast-iron frying pan to medium–high and brush with 1 tablespoon of the olive oil.

Drizzle the mackerel fillets with the remaining olive oil, then season well with salt and brush on some of the reserved dressing. Place the fish on the grill, skin side down, and cook for 2–3 minutes, until the skin is crispy, brushing occasionally with the reserved dressing. Turn the fish over and grill for another 2–3 minutes, again basting with the dressing, until the fish is cooked through.

To build your burgers, slather the bun bases with lemon yoghurt sauce. Add the salad, a mackerel fillet and drizzle with any remaining dressing. Finish with the bun tops and serve with lemon wedges.

NOTES

Aleppo pepper is a moderately spicy chilli pepper with a complex fruity, tangy flavour that is popular in Middle Eastern cuisine.

A cousin of Aleppo pepper, the Maras biber chilli is grown in the Maras region between Turkey and Syria and has a peppery, fruity flavour with a gentle lingering heat.

Urfa biber hails from the Urfa region in Turkey and has a smoky, raisin-like taste and mild chilli bite.

You can buy these peppers online, and from spice shops and specialist grocers. If you can't find all three, just use Aleppo pepper.

THE NEW ENGLAND LOBSTER

500 g (1 lb 2 oz) cooked lobster meat

125 g (½ cup) Mayonnaise (page 16)

2 teaspoons chopped chives

1 tablespoon chopped dill fronds

1 large spring onion (scallion), finely sliced

zest of 1 lemon

2–3 teaspoons lemon juice

2 teaspoons baby capers, rinsed

good pinch of hot paprika

splash of Tabasco sauce, plus extra (optional)

sea salt and cracked black pepper

TO SERVE

4 potato buns or brioche buns, lightly toasted and buttered

butter lettuce leaves

8 slices crispy bacon (optional)

8 tomato slices

1 avocado, sliced

chopped chives

Dice the lobster meat into bite-sized pieces. Place the mayonnaise in a bowl with the chives, dill, spring onion, lemon zest, lemon juice, capers, paprika and Tabasco sauce and whisk to combine. Toss the lobster meat through, then season to taste with salt, pepper and a little more Tabasco, if desired.

To build your burgers, layer the base buns with a few lettuce leaves, two bacon slices, if using, two tomato slices, some avocado, and plenty of the creamy lobster. Add a sprinkling of chopped chives, then finish with the bun tops and enjoy.

AHI TUNA SUSHI

RICE BUNS

330 g (1½ cups) sushi rice

2 tablespoons sake

2 tablespoons rice vinegar

4½ teaspoons sugar

pinch of sea salt

TO COOK THE RICE BUNS

125 g (1 cup) cornflour (corn starch)

2 large eggs

180 g (3 cups) panko breadcrumbs

2 teaspoons black sesame seeds

2 teaspoons white sesame seeds

peanut oil, for shallow-frying

TUNA SUSHI

450 g (1 lb) sashimi-grade ahi tuna, diced into 1 cm (½ in) chunks

40 ml (1¼ fl oz) soy sauce

4 teaspoons rice wine vinegar

1 tablespoon toasted sesame oil

1½ teaspoons finely grated ginger

1 spring onion (scallion), very finely sliced

1 teaspoon shichimi togarashi

TO SERVE

sriracha mayonnaise

2 handfuls of Asian salad leaves

1 small carrot, finely julienned

1 short cucumber, finely sliced into ribbons

1 large avocado, finely sliced

2 tablespoons tobiko (flying fish roe) or salmon roe

Rinse the rice under cold running water until the water runs clear, then soak the rice in a bowl of cold water for 25 minutes. Drain and place in a saucepan with 375 ml (1½ cups) of fresh water. Bring to the boil over high heat, then immediately reduce to a low simmer. Cover and cook for about 10 minutes, until the water has been absorbed. Remove from the heat, keeping the lid on, and sit for a further 10 minutes.

Meanwhile, place the sake, rice vinegar, sugar and salt in a small saucepan and stir over low heat until the sugar has dissolved.

Turn the rested rice out into a large bowl, pour the warm sake mixture over and gently fold through to combine, until the rice is cooled slightly.

Line a large baking tray with baking paper. Divide the rice into eight equal portions. Place a 10 cm (4 in) round cookie cutter on the baking paper and fill with a portion of sushi rice. Using the back of a spoon, firmly press the rice into the ring. Continue with the remaining rice until you have eight 'bun' halves. Cover with baking paper, place another tray on top to weigh the buns down and refrigerate for 3 hours.

When ready to cook the rice buns, set up a dredging station with three large shallow bowls. Place the cornflour in one bowl, whisk the eggs in a second bowl, and in the third bowl combine the panko crumbs and black and white sesame seeds. Place the buns, one at a time, in the cornflour and turn to evenly coat. Dip them in the egg, turning to completely coat, then into the sesame panko crumbs, pressing the crumbs and seeds into the buns.

Pour about 2.5 cm (1 in) of peanut oil into a large deep frying pan and heat to 185ºC (365ºF) over medium heat. Working in batches, carefully place the rice buns into the hot oil and fry for 1–2 minutes on each side, until golden brown and crispy. Transfer to a wire rack lined with paper towel to absorb the excess oil and cool.

Place all the tuna sushi ingredients in a bowl and toss to combine. To build your burgers, drizzle some sriracha mayonnaise on four of the rice buns and top with Asian salad leaves, carrot, cucumber ribbons, avocado slices and the tuna sushi mixture. Add the tobiko and some more sriracha mayonnaise and finish with the remaining rice buns.

CRAB WITH TARTAR SAUCE

SEAFOOD

550 g (1 lb 3 oz) cooked, cleaned lump crabmeat

150 g (1½ cups) crushed saltine crackers

1 celery stalk, finely diced

1 large spring onion (scallion), finely sliced

1 tablespoon chopped parsley

1 tablespoon chopped dill fronds

1 tablespoon chopped chives

1 egg, beaten

zest of ½ lemon

60 g (¼ cup) Mayonnaise (page 16)

2 teaspoons dijon mustard

2 teaspoons Old Bay Seasoning

½ teaspoon fine sea salt

½ teaspoon cracked black pepper

1–1½ teaspoons hot sauce, such as Franks, to taste (optional)

125 ml (½ cup) peanut oil, for shallow-frying

TO SERVE

4 brioche buns, lightly toasted and buttered

dijonnaise

handful of watercress

1 baby fennel bulb, finely sliced

¼ cup dill fronds

¼ cup parsley leaves

½ lemon, plus lemon wedges

¼ red onion, finely sliced

Tartar sauce (page 17)

Place the crabmeat in a large bowl with 50 g (½ cup) of the cracker crumbs. Add the celery, spring onion, herbs, egg, lemon zest, mayonnaise, mustard, Old Bay Seasoning, salt, pepper and hot sauce, if using. Mix well to combine, then evenly shape into four patties slightly larger than your buns.

Spread the remaining cracker crumbs in a shallow bowl and coat the crab patties, covering them completely. Place on a tray lined with baking paper, then cover and chill in the fridge for 45–60 minutes.

Heat a cast-iron frying pan over medium heat and pour in 60 ml (¼ cup) of the peanut oil. When hot, cook two of the crab patties for 3–4 minutes on each side, until golden brown and crispy. Repeat with the remaining crab patties and oil, then remove to a plate and keep warm.

To build your burgers, slather the base buns with dijonnaise. Toss the watercress, fennel, parsley and most of the dill fronds together in a bowl, squeeze the ½ lemon over and toss to combine. Add the salad to the buns, then top with a crab burger, the onion slices, a dollop of tartar sauce and the remaining dill fronds. Finish with the bun tops and serve with lemon wedges on the side.

BAJA FRIED FISH

SEAFOOD

600 g (1 lb 5 oz) firm white fish fillets, sliced into 8 even pieces (about 75 g/2½ oz each)

sea salt flakes

60 g (½ cup) cornflour (corn starch)

150 g (1 cup) plain (all-purpose) flour

½ teaspoon baking soda

1 teaspoon chilli powder

½ teaspoon onion powder

½ teaspoon garlic powder

½ teaspoon cracked black pepper

1 egg

250 ml (1 cup) Mexican beer or pale ale

peanut oil, for deep-frying

JALAPENO LIME DRESSING

60 g (¼ cup) Mayonnaise (page 16)

60 g (¼ cup) Mexican crema or sour cream

2 tablespoons chopped pickled jalapeno chillies

1–2 teaspoons jalapeno chilli pickle juice (from the jar)

zest and juice of 1 lime

TO SERVE

4 sesame seed hamburger buns, lightly toasted and buttered

chipotle mayonnaise (store-bought)

3 handfuls of finely shredded red cabbage

½ red onion, finely sliced

handful of coriander (cilantro) leaves

guacamole

lime wedges

Place the jalapeno lime dressing ingredients in a small bowl, whisk to combine and set aside. The dressing will keep in a sealed glass jar in the fridge for up to 5 days.

Season the fish with salt flakes, dust well with the cornflour and set aside.

In a bowl, whisk together the plain flour, baking soda and spices. Add the egg and beer and whisk again until smooth.

Pour about 7.5 cm (3 in) of peanut oil into a large deep frying pan or saucepan and heat to 180ºC (350ºF) over medium heat.

One at a time, dip the fish pieces into the beer batter, shaking off the excess, and carefully lower into the hot oil. Fry the fish in batches, taking care not to overcrowd the pan, for about 2 minutes on each side, until golden brown and cooked through. Transfer to a wire rack lined with paper towel to absorb the excess oil. Sprinkle with salt flakes.

To build your burgers, slather the base buns with chipotle mayo, then add some cabbage, red onion, coriander leaves and a drizzle of the jalapeno lime dressing. Next, add a dollop of guacamole and two pieces of fish, then drizzle over a little more dressing and chipotle mayo. Finish with the bun tops and serve with lime wedges.

CRISPY SKIN SALMON WITH SWEET & SPICY CUCUMBER SALAD

SEAFOOD

sea salt flakes

1 tablespoon olive oil

SALMON PATTIES

4 skin-on wild-caught salmon fillets, about 500 g (1 lb 2 oz) in total, deboned

1 egg, beaten

25 g (1 oz) panko breadcrumbs

2 tablespoons roughly chopped coriander (cilantro) leaves

1 garlic clove, minced

1 small makrut lime leaf, tough centre rib discarded, shredded

1½ tablespoons lime juice

2 teaspoons finely grated ginger

2 teaspoons diced green chilli

2 teaspoons Thai red curry paste

SWEET & SPICY CUCUMBER SALAD

165 g (6 oz) cucumber, halved lengthways, seeds scooped out, finely sliced

¼ small red onion, finely sliced

small handful of coriander (cilantro) leaves

1 tablespoon crushed salted roasted peanuts

2 teaspoons lime juice

2 teaspoons rice wine vinegar

1 teaspoon sweet chilli sauce

1 teaspoon sesame oil

1 teaspoon finely chopped red chilli

½ teaspoon fish sauce

TO SERVE

2 handfuls of shaved white cabbage

4 sesame seed brioche buns, lightly toasted and buttered

sriracha mayonnaise

sweet chilli sauce (optional)

lime cheeks

To make the salmon patties, remove the skin from each salmon fillet using a thin sharp knife and set aside. Roughly dice the flesh and place in a food processor with the remaining ingredients. Pulse just a few times until the mixture comes together, taking care not to overmix. Shape into four even patties, slightly bigger than your buns. Use your thumb to make a small indentation in the centre of each patty, to help them retain their shape during cooking and prevent doming. Cover and refrigerate for 20–30 minutes to firm up.

Generously sprinkle both sides of the reserved salmon skins with salt flakes, then place on a tray and refrigerate for 40 minutes, or up to 1 hour. Do not cover them, as you want the cold air to dry out the skin.

Combine all the sweet and spicy cucumber salad ingredients in a bowl, tossing well. Cover and refrigerate until ready to use.

When ready to cook, place a cast-iron frying pan over medium heat and, when hot, add the olive oil. Add the salmon skins and cook, using a spatula to press them flat, for about 2 minutes on each side, until crispy. Transfer to a wire rack lined with paper towel to absorb the excess oil.

Sprinkle both sides of the salmon patties with salt flakes and add to the hot pan. Cook for 2½–3 minutes on each side, until golden brown and done to your liking.

To build your burgers, pile the cabbage on the base buns and drizzle with sriracha mayonnaise. Add the salmon burgers, a drizzle of sweet chilli sauce, if using, and the cucumber salad. Top with the crispy salmon skin and finish with the bun tops. Serve with lime cheeks.

THE TUNA MELT

SEAFOOD

425 g (15 oz) tinned tuna in olive oil, drained

125 g (½ cup) Kewpie mayonnaise

1 tablespoon dijon mustard

3 tablespoons sweet pickle relish

3 tablespoons finely diced red onion

3 tablespoons chopped dill fronds

1 celery stalk, finely diced

1–2 tablespoons chopped pickled jalapeno chillies, to taste

2 teaspoons salted baby capers, rinsed

1 tablespoon lemon juice

sea salt and cracked black pepper

60 g (2 oz) salted butter, softened

4 hamburger buns, split

8 slices American-style cheese

TO SERVE

salted potato chips (crisps)

cornichons

Place the tuna in a large bowl and use a fork to flake the fish into smaller pieces. Add the mayonnaise, mustard, pickle relish, onion, dill, celery, jalapeno chilli and capers. Mix well to combine, then add the lemon juice and salt and pepper to taste.

Preheat the grill (broiler) to medium–high. Warm a cast-iron frying pan over medium heat.

Butter the inside of the hamburger buns, both top and bottom. Working in batches, toast the buns, buttered side down, in the frying pan for a few minutes, until golden brown and toasty. Place them on a baking tray, toasted side facing up.

Place a slice of cheese on each bun half, then grill for 1–2 minutes to melt the cheese. Remove from the grill.

To build your burgers, spread the tuna mixture on the four base buns, then top with a handful of potato chips. Finish with the cheesy bun tops and serve with extra chips and cornichons on the side.

HALOUMI WITH ROASTED RED PEPPER & SALSA VERDE

VEGETARIAN & VEGAN

1 large red bell pepper (capsicum),
cut into 8 slices, seeds discarded

1 zucchini (courgette), cut diagonally
into 5 mm (¼ in) thick slices

2 tablespoons olive oil

2 tablespoons finely chopped
parsley leaves

2 garlic cloves, minced

1 teaspoon lemon zest

good pinch of chilli flakes

sea salt and cracked black pepper

4 × 100 g (3½ oz) haloumi slices,
each about 1 cm (½ in) thick

½ lemon

SALSA VERDE

1½ cups parsley leaves

1 cup basil leaves

2 garlic cloves, peeled

1 tablespoon salted baby capers, rinsed

juice of ½ lemon, plus extra (optional)

good pinch of chilli flakes

125 ml (½ cup) extra virgin olive oil,
plus extra (optional)

sea salt and cracked black pepper

TO SERVE

4 ciabatta rolls, lightly toasted
and buttered

Tzatziki (page 24)

2 handfuls of rocket (arugula)

½ red onion, finely sliced

2 tablespoons pomegranate seeds

2 tablespoons chopped pistachios

To make the salsa verde, place the parsley, basil and garlic in a food processor, along with the capers, lemon juice and chilli flakes. Blitz to combine. With the motor running, add the olive oil and process to your desired texture. If you prefer a thinner salsa, add a little more oil. Taste and season with salt, pepper and more lemon juice, if desired, and set aside. The salsa will keep in a sealed glass jar in the fridge for 5–7 days.

Place the bell pepper and zucchini slices in a shallow dish with the olive oil, parsley, garlic, lemon zest and chilli flakes. Season with salt and pepper and toss well to coat.

Heat a cast-iron frying pan or chargrill pan over medium heat. Working in batches, grill the bell pepper and zucchini slices for about 2 minutes on each side, until tender. Transfer to a platter and keep warm.

Grill the haloumi slices for 3–4 minutes on each side, until golden brown and charred with grill marks. Squeeze the lemon juice over and season with cracked black pepper.

To build your burgers, slather the base rolls with tzatziki, then add some rocket, grilled red pepper and zucchini, red onion slices, a slice of grilled haloumi and a drizzle of salsa verde. Top with a sprinkling of pomegranate seeds and pistachios, then finish with more salsa verde and the bun tops.

CHIPOTLE BLACK BEAN

45 g (¾ cup) panko breadcrumbs, for coating

60 ml (¼ cup) olive oil

4 slices vegan American-style cheese

BLACK BEAN PATTIES

400 g (14 oz) tin black beans, rinsed (drained weight 220 g/8 oz)

60 g (2 oz) roughly chopped onion

15 g (½ oz) rolled (porridge) oats

2 teaspoons chopped chipotle chillies in adobo sauce

2 teaspoons tamari

1 teaspoon maple syrup

1 teaspoon dijon mustard

1 teaspoon tahini

½ teaspoon smoked paprika

½ teaspoon ground cumin

½ teaspoon vegan stock powder

40 g (1½ oz) panko breadcrumbs

VEGAN CHIPOTLE CREMA

250 g (1 cup) vegan sour cream

2 chipotle chillies in adobo sauce, plus 2–3 teaspoons of the adobo sauce

1 tablespoon lime juice

TO SERVE

4 rye hamburger buns, lightly toasted

2 handfuls of rocket (arugula)

guacamole

Pickled red onion (page 21)

sliced pickled jalapeno chillies

Place all the black bean patty ingredients, except the panko crumbs, in a food processor. Pulse just until the mixture holds together when squeezed. Now add the panko crumbs and pulse to just combine; do not overmix.

Divide the mixture into four equal portions and shape into patties. Place the panko crumbs for coating in a shallow bowl, add the patties and turn to coat all over, ensuring they are completely covered. Place on a baking tray lined with baking paper, then cover and leave to set in the fridge for about 20 minutes.

Meanwhile, place all the vegan chipotle crema ingredients in a small blender and blitz to your desired consistency. Set aside. The crema will keep in a sealed glass jar in the fridge for about 5 days.

Warm the olive oil in a cast-iron frying pan set over medium–high heat. Carefully place the patties in the pan and cook for about 3 minutes, until well browned and crispy. Flip them over and cook for a further 2 minutes.

Turn off the heat, top each patty with a slice of cheese, and cover the pan with a lid. The residual heat will finish cooking the patty and melt the cheese.

To build your burgers, smear the base buns with the chipotle crema, then top with rocket, guacamole, a burger patty, some pickled red onion and a few slices of pickled jalapeno chilli. Drizzle with more crema and finish with the bun tops.

SESAME TOFU WITH CHILLI PEANUT SLAW

VEGETARIAN & VEGAN

650 g (1 lb 7 oz) extra-firm tofu, sliced into 4 thick slabs, each about 2 cm (¾ in) thick

peanut oil, for shallow-frying

TOFU MARINADE

60 g (2 oz) gochujang paste

2 tablespoons soy sauce or tamari

3 tablespoons maple syrup or honey

1 tablespoon rice wine vinegar

1 tablespoon toasted sesame oil

1 tablespoon finely grated ginger

3 garlic cloves, minced

CHILLI PEANUT SLAW

225 g (3 cups) shredded cabbage

2 spring onions (scallions), finely sliced

2 tablespoons chopped roasted peanuts

60 g (¼ cup) sriracha mayonnaise

1–2 teaspoons rice vinegar

TOFU BATTER

75 g (2¾ oz) brown rice flour

125 ml (½ cup) soy milk or water

1 teaspoon baking powder

CRUMB COATING

60 g (1 cup) panko breadcrumbs

2 tablespoons sesame seeds

good pinch of sea salt

SPICY SAUCE

80 ml (⅓ cup) reserved tofu marinade (see above)

2 tablespoons ketchup

1 tablespoon maple syrup or honey

TO SERVE

4 hamburger buns, lightly toasted

Kewpie mayonnaise

Pat the tofu dry with paper towel, pressing out the excess moisture. Place the tofu in a large container.

In a bowl, whisk together all the tofu marinade ingredients. Pour the marinade over the tofu and turn to coat, completely covering the tofu. Cover and leave in the fridge for about 2 hours to allow the tofu to absorb the flavours.

Meanwhile, place all the slaw ingredients in a large bowl and toss to combine.

Place the batter ingredients in a bowl and whisk together. In a separate bowl, mix together the crumb coating ingredients.

Remove the tofu from the marinade, reserving about 80 ml (⅓ cup) of the marinade for the spicy sauce. Dip the tofu into the batter, turning to coat completely. Shake off the excess batter, then coat the tofu with the crumb coating, pressing the crumbs onto the tofu so they adhere well. Allow to sit while the oil is heating up.

Pour 1.5 cm (½ in) of peanut oil into a frying pan set over medium–high heat.

Meanwhile, make the spicy sauce. Place the reserved marinade in a small saucepan with the ketchup and maple syrup. Simmer for a few minutes over medium–high heat, stirring until combined. Add a tablespoon of water if you'd like a thinner sauce. Set aside.

When the peanut oil is hot, cook the tofu for about 1½ minutes on each side, until golden and crunchy. Transfer to a wire rack lined with paper towel to absorb the excess oil.

To build your burgers, slather the base buns with mayo, top with the slaw and a slab of fried tofu, then drizzle with the spicy sauce. Slather more mayonnaise on the inside of the bun tops, place them on the burgers and enjoy.

FRIED GREEN TOMATO WITH TABASCO AIOLI

VEGETARIAN & VEGAN

1 egg

80 ml (⅓ cup) buttermilk

1 teaspoon Cajun seasoning

35 g (¼ cup) plain (all-purpose) flour

50 g (⅓ cup) cornmeal

30 g (½ cup) panko breadcrumbs

2 tablespoons finely grated parmesan

½ teaspoon sea salt

½ teaspoon cracked black pepper

¼ teaspoon cayenne pepper

2 large unripe green tomatoes, cut into 4 slices about 1–1.5 cm (½ in) thick

vegetable oil, for shallow-frying

sea salt flakes

TABASCO AIOLI

125 g (½ cup) Mayonnaise (page 16)

2 garlic cloves, minced

1 tablespoon lemon juice

1 tablespoon Tabasco, or to taste

¼ teaspoon cracked black pepper

TO SERVE

4 potato buns or onion rolls, lightly toasted and buttered

handful of rocket (arugula)

8 slices crispy plant-based 'bacon'

4 fried eggs

tomato chutney

Place all the tabasco aioli ingredients in a small bowl and whisk to combine, then set aside. The aioli will keep in an airtight container in the fridge for 5–7 days.

Set up your 'crumbing' station. In a shallow bowl, whisk together the egg, buttermilk and ½ teaspoon of the Cajun seasoning. Place the flour in a separate shallow bowl. In a third shallow bowl, combine the cornmeal, panko crumbs, parmesan, salt, pepper, cayenne pepper and remaining ½ teaspoon of Cajun seasoning, whisking well.

Dip the tomato slices into the egg mixture, then the flour, then back into the egg mixture for a second dip. Finish with the seasoned breadcrumbs, pressing the crumbs into the tomato slices to make sure they adhere well.

Pour about 2.5 cm (1 in) of vegetable oil into a cast-iron frying pan and heat to 185ºC (365ºF) over medium heat.

Working in batches, carefully place the crumbed tomato slices into the oil and cook for 2–3 minutes on each side, until lightly golden brown and crunchy. Transfer to a wire rack lined with paper towel to absorb the excess oil and season with a good sprinkling of salt flakes.

To build your burgers, slather the Tabasco aioli on the base buns. Top with rocket, two 'bacon' slices, a fried green tomato slice and a fried egg. Add a dollop of tomato chutney to the bun tops, then add to the burgers and enjoy.

THE CALIFORNIAN

VEGETARIAN & VEGAN

425 g (15 oz) tin lentils, rinsed
(drained weight 200 g/7 oz)

150 g (5½ oz) roasted pumpkin
(winter squash)

100 g (3½ oz) cooked quinoa
(about ½ cup)

80 g (2¾ oz) cooked chickpeas
(garbanzo beans) (about ½ cup)

50 g (½ cup) rolled (porridge) oats

35 g (⅓ cup) walnuts, toasted
and finely chopped

2 tablespoons panko breadcrumbs

2 garlic cloves, minced

1 teaspoon sea salt

1 teaspoon smoked paprika

½ teaspoon cracked black pepper

½ teaspoon onion powder

½ teaspoon ground cumin

olive oil, for drizzling

TO SERVE

4 wholemeal (whole-wheat)
or seeded hamburger buns, lightly
toasted

Mayonnaise (page 16)

2 handfuls of rocket (arugula)

1 avocado, sliced

Pickled red onion (page 21)

Green goddess dressing (page 20)

alfalfa or pea shoot sprouts

spiced or toasted pumpkin seeds
(pepitas)

Combine the lentils, pumpkin, quinoa and chickpeas in a bowl and roughly mash together. Add the oats, walnuts, panko crumbs, garlic, salt and spices and mix well to combine. Divide the mixture into four equal portions and shape into patties about 2.5 cm (1 in) thick. Pop the patties into the fridge for 15–20 minutes to firm up.

Meanwhile, preheat the oven to 190°C (375°F).

Place the burger patties on a lightly oiled baking tray, then drizzle with a little olive oil and season with sea salt. Bake for 10–12 minutes on each side, until nicely browned and heated through.

To build your burgers, slather the base buns with mayo and add the rocket. Top with the patties, avocado, pickled red onion, green goddess dressing, sprouts and a sprinkling of pumpkin seeds. Finish with the bun tops and enjoy.

SAUCY BARBECUE JACKFRUIT

1 tablespoon olive oil

½ onion, finely sliced

2 garlic cloves, minced

2 × 500 g (1 lb 2 oz) tins jackfruit, drained and rinsed

125–185 ml (½–¾ cup) vegan barbecue sauce (depending on how saucy you like it)

VEGAN SLAW

300 g (4 cups) finely sliced red cabbage

1 carrot, grated

90 g (⅓ cup) vegan mayonnaise

2–3 teaspoons apple cider vinegar

sea salt and cracked black pepper

TO SERVE

4 sesame seed hamburger buns, lightly toasted

vegan mayonnaise

sliced dill pickles and whole dill pickles

Warm the olive oil in a frying pan over medium–low heat and cook the onion and garlic for 5–7 minutes, until softened. Add the jackfruit and barbecue sauce and cook for 15–20 minutes, stirring occasionally, until reduced and sticky, stirring in 1–2 tablespoons of water if needed for a saucy consistency. While the sauce is simmering, you can use two forks to pull and shred the jackfruit into smaller pieces, if desired.

To make the slaw, toss the cabbage, carrot, mayonnaise and vinegar in a bowl. Mix well and season to taste with salt and pepper.

To build your burgers, slather the base buns with mayonnaise. Top with the saucy barbecue jackfruit, then the slaw and sliced pickles. Finish with the bun tops and serve with whole pickles on the side.

DOUBLE IMPOSSIBLE 'CHEESE'

VEGETARIAN & VEGAN

1 tablespoon olive oil

8 'Beyond' or 'Impossible' burger patties (store bought)

8 slices vegan American-style cheese

VEGAN SPECIAL SAUCE

125 g (½ cup) vegan mayonnaise

2 tablespoons ketchup

2 tablespoons sweet pickle relish, or to taste

1 tablespoon American mustard

½ teaspoon white vinegar

½ teaspoon smoked paprika

¼ teaspoon garlic powder

¼ teaspoon onion powder

pinch of cayenne pepper (optional)

TO SERVE

4 vegan sesame seed hamburger buns, lightly toasted

vegan mayonnaise

2 large handfuls of shredded iceberg or cos (romaine) lettuce

8 juicy tomato slices

½ red onion, finely sliced into rings

sliced dill pickles

American mustard (optional)

Place all the special sauce ingredients in a bowl and whisk to combine, then set aside. The sauce will keep in a sealed glass jar in the fridge for 7–10 days.

Warm the olive oil in a frying pan over medium heat. Cook the patties for 3–4 minutes on each side, or according to the packet instructions. For the final minute of cooking, place a slice of cheese on each patty, cover with a lid and allow to melt.

To build your burgers, slather the base buns with vegan mayonnaise. Top with a good handful of shredded lettuce, two tomato slices, two cheese-topped burger patties and the sliced red onion and dill pickles. Drizzle over a generous quantity of special sauce, then spread some mustard or more mayonnaise on the inside of the bun tops. Place them on the burgers and serve.

EGGPLANT PARMIGIANA WITH SCAMORZA

VEGETARIAN & VEGAN

1 large eggplant (aubergine),
or 2 medium-sized ones

2 eggs

120 g (2 cups) panko breadcrumbs

3 tablespoons finely grated parmesan,
plus extra for sprinkling

2 teaspoons dried Italian
herb seasoning

½ teaspoon sea salt

½ teaspoon cracked black pepper

½ teaspoon garlic powder

3–4 tablespoons olive oil

8 slices scamorza (smoked
mozzarella)

TO SERVE

1 garlic clove, halved

4 focaccia or ciabatta-style buns,
lightly toasted and buttered

250 g (1 cup) Napoli sauce (page 25),
warmed

chilli flakes

basil leaves

large handful of rocket (arugula)

Preheat the oven to 200°C (400°F).

Slice the eggplant into eight rounds, each about 1.5 cm (½ inch) thick.

Set up your crumbing station with two shallow bowls. In one bowl, whisk the eggs; in the second bowl, mix together the panko crumbs, parmesan, dried herbs, salt, pepper and garlic powder.

Dip the eggplant slices, one at a time, into the egg, then dredge through the seasoned crumbs, coating well and pressing the crumbs on so they adhere to the eggplant. Set the crumbed eggplant aside on a wire rack, ready for cooking.

Heat the olive oil in a large cast-iron frying pan over medium heat. Working in batches, cook the eggplant slices for about 2½ minutes on each side, until golden brown, crunchy and cooked through. Return each batch to the wire rack.

Place the wire rack on a baking tray lined with baking paper. Top the eggplant with a slice of scamorza and some extra grated parmesan. Pop into the oven and bake for 1–2 minutes, until the cheese has melted.

To build your burgers, rub the garlic halves across the inside of the toasted buns to impart some garlicky flavour. Spread some napoli sauce on the base buns, then top each with two cheesy eggplant slices, some chilli flakes, basil leaves and rocket. Finish with the bun tops and enjoy.

MAKES 6

BOMBAY BURGER WITH RAITA

VEGETARIAN & VEGAN

500 g (1 lb 2 oz) potatoes, skin on

4 teaspoons extra virgin coconut oil

½ teaspoon brown mustard seeds

12 fresh curry leaves

2.5 cm (1 in) piece of ginger, peeled and very finely grated

3 garlic cloves, minced

1 long green chilli, finely chopped

½ teaspoon ground turmeric

1 teaspoon sea salt

3 tablespoons chopped coriander (cilantro) leaves

peanut oil, for deep-frying

BATTER

110 g (1 cup) chickpea flour (besan)

½ teaspoon Kashmiri chilli powder

½ teaspoon ground cumin

¼ teaspoon ground turmeric

⅛ teaspoon baking soda

TO SERVE

coriander chutney (see Note)

6 small bap rolls, lightly toasted and buttered

crispy fried shallots (store bought)

mint and coriander (cilantro) sprigs

Pickled red onion (page 21)

Cucumber raita (page 24)

dry coconut chutney (see Note)

12 green chillies, grilled

Boil the potatoes in salted boiling water for 18–20 minutes, until tender when pierced with a fork. Drain and peel, then roughly chop and set aside in a large bowl.

Warm the coconut oil in a saucepan over medium heat. Add the mustard seeds and wait for a minute until they begin to pop, then add the curry leaves and saute together for another minute. Add the ginger, garlic, chilli and turmeric and saute for 1–2 minutes, until fragrant. Tip the mixture over the potatoes and lightly mash together to combine. Season with the salt. Allow to cool slightly, then add the chopped coriander and mix through. Roll the potato mixture into six equal-sized balls and set aside.

Pour about 7.5 cm (3 in) of peanut oil into a large deep frying pan or saucepan and heat to 180ºC (350ºF) over medium heat.

Meanwhile, make the batter. Place the chickpea flour, chilli powder, cumin, turmeric and baking soda in a mixing bowl and whisk to combine. Add 165 ml (5½ fl oz) of water and whisk again until smooth. The batter needs to be thick, yet thin enough to coat and cover the potato balls. If needed, add more water, a teaspoon at a time, to attain the desired consistency.

One at a time, place a potato ball in the batter, coating it completely, then remove and allow the excess to drip off. Use a slotted metal spoon to carefully lower the potato ball into the hot oil and cook for about 3 minutes, until golden brown. Transfer to a wire rack lined with paper towel to absorb the excess oil.

To build your burgers, slather some coriander chutney on the base rolls, then sprinkle with crispy fried shallots. Add a few herb sprigs, then a potato ball and some pickled red onion. Slather cucumber raita on the inside of the roll tops and scatter with coconut chutney. Add the roll tops to the burgers and serve with grilled green chillies on the side.

NOTE

Bombay burgers are typically served with dry coconut chutney, coriander chutney and sometimes tamarind chutney. You can buy these ready-made condiments from Indian and Asian grocers.

GRILLED PORTOBELLO

3 tablespoons olive oil

2 tablespoons balsamic vinegar

1–2 garlic cloves, minced

4 thyme sprigs, leaves picked

4 large portobello mushrooms, stems removed

sea salt and cracked black pepper

4 slices havarti cheese

TO SERVE

4 small kaiser rolls or hamburger buns, lightly toasted and buttered

dijonnaise

2 handfuls of mixed salad leaves

1 avocado, sliced

½ red onion, shaved into thin rings

1 tomato, sliced

zucchini (courgette) pickles

Place the olive oil, balsamic vinegar, garlic and thyme leaves in a bowl and whisk to combine. Add the mushrooms and turn to coat a few times, ensuring they are covered in the marinade. Season with salt and pepper, then set aside for about 20 minutes to allow the flavours to soak in.

Heat a cast-iron frying pan or chargrill pan over medium heat and cook the mushrooms cap side up for about 4 minutes, brushing with the marinade occasionally. Turn the mushrooms over and cook for a further 1–2 minutes. Place a slice of cheese on each mushroom, turn off the heat and cover with a lid. Leave the cheese to melt from the residual heat for about 1 minute.

To assemble your burgers, slather the base buns with dijonnaise, then top with salad leaves, avocado, the grilled mushrooms, red onion, tomato and zucchini pickles. Slather more dijonnaise on the inside of the bun tops, place them on the burgers and enjoy.

INDEX

Published in 2025 by Smith Street Books
Naarm (Melbourne) | Australia
smithstreetbooks.com

Distributed outside of ANZ, North & Latin America by
Thames & Hudson Ltd., 6–24 Britannia Street, London, WC1X 9JD
thamesandhudson.com

EU Authorized Representative: Interart S.A.R.L.
19 rue Charles Auray, 93500 Pantin, Paris, France
productsafety@thameshudson.co.uk; www.interart.fr

ISBN: 978-1-9232-3910-4

Smith Street Books respectfully acknowledges the Wurundjeri People of the Kulin Nation, who are the
Traditional Owners of the land on which we work, and we pay our respects to their Elders past and present.

Publisher: Paul McNally
Managing editor: Lucy Heaver
Editor: Katri Hilden
Design and illustrations: George Saad Studio
Typesetter: Nikola Kyle
Photography: Emily Weaving
Food styling: Deborah Kaloper
Food preparation: Caroline Griffiths and Meryl Batlle
Proofreader: Pamela Dunne
Indexer: Rachel Pitts

Printed & bound in China by C&C Offset Printing Co., Ltd.

Book 399
10 9 8 7 6 5 4 3 2 1